Outgrowing Cultic Christianity

Outgrowing Cultic Christianity

Restoring the Role of Religion

Robert P. Vande Kappelle

WIPF & STOCK · Eugene, Oregon

OUTGROWING CULTIC CHRISTIANITY
Restoring the Role of Religion

Copyright © 2021 Robert P. Vande Kappelle. All rights reserved. Except for brief quotations in critical publications or reviews, no part of this book may be reproduced in any manner without prior written permission from the publisher. Write: Permissions, Wipf and Stock Publishers, 199 W. 8th Ave., Suite 3, Eugene, OR 97401.

Unless otherwise noted, Bible quotations are from the *New Revised Standard Version of the Bible*, copyright © 1989 by the Division of Christian Education of the National Council of the Churches of Christ in the United States of America. Used by permission.

Wipf & Stock
An Imprint of Wipf and Stock Publishers
199 W. 8th Ave., Suite 3
Eugene, OR 97401

www.wipfandstock.com

PAPERBACK ISBN: 978-1-7252-9975-7
HARDCOVER ISBN: 978-1-7252-9976-4
EBOOK ISBN: 978-1-7252-9977-1

04/21/21

Contents

Preface		vii
Chapter 1	Conspiracy Theories	1
Chapter 2	Dynamics of Cult Development	12
Chapter 3	Dynamics of Faith Development	21
Chapter 4	Rethinking the Role of Religion	33
Chapter 5	Rethinking Belief in God	47
Chapter 6	Rethinking Scripture	61
Chapter 7	Rethinking Creation Theology	80
Chapter 8	Rethinking Jesus and the Incarnation	89
Chapter 9	The Historical Jesus and Apocalyptic Theology, Part I	104
Chapter 10	The Historical Jesus and Apocalyptic Theology, Part II	122
Chapter 11	Christianity after Religion	136
Chapter 12	Outgrowing Cultic Christianity	145
Appendix A	The Unfolding Drama of Faith in the Biblical Storyline	155
Appendix B	The Meaning of the Millennium: Four Views	163
Bibliography		167
Index		171

Preface

Thomas Kuhn's book *The Structure of Scientific Revolutions* popularized the term "paradigm shift." A paradigm is a set of beliefs, images, concepts, and structures that governs the way we think about something. Kuhn (1922–1996) said that paradigm change becomes necessary when the previous paradigm becomes so outmoded or unworkable that a complete overhaul is necessary. The shift in thinking that might have felt threatening at one time now appears as the only way forward and as a real lifeline. We could well be at one of these critical junctures today. Might we be willing to adopt a new set of values, systems, and even beliefs that could change and possibly save humanity and our world?

Some religious scholars, affirming the centrality and power of stories to the religious enterprise, are using the language of a "framing story" to describe the same phenomenon Kuhn addressed. According to Brian McLaren, a framing story "gives people direction, values, vision, and inspiration by providing a framework for their lives. It tells them who they are, where they come from, where they are, what's going on, where things are going, and what they should do."[1] While we all have stories that answer those questions on a personal level, a "framing story" dictates the general beliefs of a culture, nation, religion, and even humanity as a whole. This book calls for a paradigm shift within Christianity, a rethinking of core values and beliefs such as its doctrine of God, creation, Jesus, incarnation, and its apocalyptic theology.

According to anthropologists, the religious impetus in human beings emerged from a nondualist mindset, that is, out of human desire to affirm and safeguard cosmic unity, a sense of belonging and integration innate to Reality. To this end, stories are told—myths, we call them. Stories set the inner life into motion, and this is particularly important when

1. McLaren, *Everything Must Change*, 5–6.

the inner life is frightened or under threat. Stories help us make sense of life; they show us our way out or through life's challenges, opening doors that lead to love and learning. Such stories have the power to change our hearts and minds, further enlivening our imagination.

According to Swiss psychiatrist Carl Jung (1875–1961) and the American Joseph Campbell (1904–1997), who most developed the power of myth for our generation, human transformation only happens in the presence of story, myth, and image, and not through rational argumentation. For Christians, the formative storyline is that found in the Bible, beginning with creation, finding its midpoint in the life of Jesus, and culminating in the afterlife, when people of faith are removed from this evil world and taken to a perfect, pristine place known as heaven, where God lives and with whom we will dwell forever. Many American Christians read the story literally and traditionally, whereby Jesus comes to divide humans between the saved and the lost, the good and the bad, the sheep and the goats.

Read this way, this storyline is essentially dualistic, and for an increasing number of Christians today, dualism doesn't work. They find it counterintuitive and counterproductive. Instead, they understand the map of Jesus' life to be the map of humanity: his life is our life, a cycle of birth, identity, victories, setbacks, betrayal, death, and new life. In the end, life comes full circle: we return where we started, though now transformed. Unfortunately, this mythological, metaphorical, humanistic, and nondualistic way of understanding Jesus is not accepted by a great many Americans, and hence, the great religious divide in America today.

Jung saw the nondualist pattern repeated in every human life. He called it the Christ Archetype, an image that maps the journey of human transformation. Jung's notion of an archetype or Ruling Image helps us to understand the "Universal Stand-In" that Jesus was meant to be. Sadly, for most Christians, Jesus ended up being an exclusive Savior for us to worship instead of our inclusive Savior with whom we are joined in common humanity.

While most Christians are familiar with the Jesus' story, together with its official theological implications, more Christians are embracing the archetypal storyline. If more Americans believed it and surrendered to it, they would be happier individually and America would be more unified politically and socially, because this Christ map holds deep and unconscious integrating power for us as individuals and for society as a whole.

A Great Story connects our individual lives in the One Great Life, and even better, it finds a way to use the wounded and seemingly "unworthy" parts of our lives and others' lives for the common good (see 1 Cor 12:23). What a transformative message we have here! No wonder the early Christians called it gospel, that is, "good news." Like good art, a cosmic myth like the gospel gives humans a sense of belonging, meaning, and, most importantly, a personal participation in that storyline.

Building on a model of faith development devised by Brian McLaren, this book examines the truth of key biblical teachings. Unfortunately, many of these teachings are based upon ancient hopes and fears rather than upon factual historical information. Taken literally, dualistic biblical teachings concerning heaven and hell, sin and salvation, good and evil, and beliefs such as the deity of Jesus, his ability to perform miracles, and his imminent return to consummate God's kingdom on earth are questionable, not only because they are beyond historical and scientific verification, but also because they can be misused by authoritarian personalities to control and mislead devout individuals.

As we rethink Christian beliefs about God, scripture, creation, Jesus, incarnation, the kingdom of God, and the Second Coming of Christ, we will examine the influence of dualistic thinking upon early Christianity and its bewildering effect on American Christians. We will indicate how inadequate faith development prevents people from growing intellectually, emotionally, and spiritually, making them susceptible to disinformation and vulnerable to authoritarian personalities and cultic mindsets.

While biblical thinking can be negative and pessimistic, it can also be illuminating. Biblical literature "pulls back the curtain" to reveal what is real, true, and lasting. This is the gift not only of this literature but also of the painful experiences of our time. Biblical teaching shocks us out of what we take for granted as normal and helps us to see more clearly the purpose of life. While the biblical storyline originally pointed to the imminent end of the world, today it helps us to rethink the end of our world as we know it. This doesn't mean that life doesn't continue, only that our lives won't go the way we thought they would, could, or even should. Modified and updated to modern times and to our circumstances, religious truth encourages us to let go of previous securities and boundaries that no longer work or appear relevant.

Questions for Discussion and Reflection

1. If you were asked to reduce your core religious beliefs to three, what would they be?
2. Do you have a "framing story"? If so, state it in one or two sentences.
3. Explain the difference between reading the biblical storyline dualistically or nondualistically.
4. How would you respond to someone who asked you for your understanding of biblical or religious truth? In your estimation, is religious truth verifiable? Explain your answer.

Chapter 1

Conspiracy Theories

SOMETHING HAPPENED DURING THE first two decades of the twenty-first century that baffles the imagination, for during that period, increasingly large numbers of Americans began to espouse conspiracy theories. By conspiracy theory, I mean a theory that explains an event or a set of circumstances as the result of a secret plot, usually by powerful conspirators. Pundits once spoke of conspiracy theory thinking in America as coming from a minority of Americans, a group dubbed a "lunatic fringe," but by the end of 2020, coinciding with the end of the Trump presidency, an unprecedented number of Americans began espousing conspiracy theories, their actions and beliefs guided and controlled by such ideology.

Conspiracy theories are not new. They have existed on and off throughout history, but their effect on people has been perceived as minimal or short lasting. Conspiracy thinking is, however, pervasive in America today, to such an extent that we seem to be living in the golden age of conspiracy theories. Current conspiracy theories are not simply restricted to a fringe population, however, for at least 50 percent of Americans today are said to believe in at least one conspiracy theory, ranging from the idea that the 9/11 attacks were fake, to the birther movement, the belief that former President Barak Obama was not born in the U.S. and was possibly a Muslim plant in America by a foreign government bent on destroying American democracy.

Such theories include belief in nonhuman aliens, a feature of belief in extraterrestrial interference on our planet, a conviction often related to UFO sightings and UFO cults in the United States. Some of these theories are political in nature, such as the belief that the assassinations of

Martin Luther King, Jr. and President John F. Kennedy were not the work of lone individuals but part of a larger plot. In the United States today there are millions—perhaps tens of millions—of adults who believe that the government, large organizations, or secretive companies are hiding essential truth from the public. One such group in the U.S., known as QAnon, espouses a widespread theory that a group of Democrats and elites in America attempted to undermine Donald Trump's presidency. This conspiracy theory dates back to 2017, when a supposed high-level government official, identified simply as "Q," posted on an anonymous online messaging board details of the inner working of the government. While QAnon started among a far-right group of individuals, it turned into a mainstream belief system for millions of conservatives and Trumpists in America. It has since evolved into claims that Donald Trump was opposed by a "deep state" cabal of satanic pedophiles and cannibals. According to an October 13, 2020 survey on conspiracy theories and the 2020 election by the Center for American Progress, one-third of Republicans who had heard of QAnon said that the conspiracy claims made about the group are accurate.[1]

Other conspiracy theories currently in circulation involve belief that a secret chamber behind Lincoln's head on South Dakota's Mount Rushmore holds government secrets, hidden treasure, or even proof of extraterrestrial beings, an idea explored in Nicholas Cage's film *National Treasure: Book of Secrets*. Some Americans believe that a research facility in Alaska is a mind-control lab; others believe that the government has implanted a microchip in the coronavirus vaccine to make it easier to control the behavior of American citizens. Yet others hold that a military complex built in the 1970s in North Dakota is related to a secret group of Illuminati because of its pyramid shape, which is a symbol of Freemasonry, the largest secret society in the world. Similar conspiracy theories exist regarding the Denver International Airport, a huge complex twice the size of Manhattan said to have been constructed billions over budget and to contain secret structures and even markers to "The New World Airport Commission," an organization unknown otherwise. Not to be outdone, some people in Idaho believe the government is poisoning them with chemicals.[2]

---

1. Cox and Halpin, "Conspiracy theories."
2. Alito, "Popular conspiracy theories in the U.S."

While dozens of similar conspiracies exist not only in America but also around the world, since the onset of the coronavirus crisis early in 2020, conspiracy theories have been spreading about as fast as the virus itself. To find out more about the acceptance and dissemination of such conspiracy theories, in June 2020, opinion researchers at Germany's Allensbach Institute surveyed one thousand representative citizens in the United States, Great Britain, France, and Germany. While 32 percent of American participants labeled conspiracy theorists "crackpots," as many as 22 percent viewed conspiracy theories as potentially credible. One in four Americans also questioned the reliability of mainstream media reporting, particularly with regard to the truth about the coronavirus epidemic, preferring to obtain information from independent sources.

In response to one of the survey items, many younger participants felt the coronavirus crisis was being exploited by a few wealthy elites "to set up a new world order." According to a September 21, 2020 survey by the University of Pennsylvania's Annenberg Public Policy Center, more than one in three Americans believe that the Chinese government engineered the coronavirus as a weapon, and another third are convinced that the Center for Disease Control and Prevention has exaggerated the threat of COVID-19 to undermine President Trump. Such beliefs may taper off as countries begin to contain the virus, but at present they underscore that a particular form of conspiracy theory is emerging in the mainstream—a belief that the "official story" is in fact a lie, told by powerful, shadowy interests. Estimates of how many Americans firmly believe at least one discredited conspiracy theory hover around 50 percent, but that may be low. To paraphrase a popular bumper sticker, if you don't think someone is plotting against you, you're not paying attention.

The American election of President Joe Biden in 2020 also fueled conspiracy theories. At a time of rising distrust in the news, internet rumors, and viral conspiracies, a national survey of more than three thousand Americans found the public ready to believe the accuracy of unproven or disproven claims. The report, a collaboration between American Enterprise Institute's Survey Center on American Life and the Center for American Progress, found "a significant number of Americans susceptible to believing unproven lies." While a majority of Democrats believe Russia aided or suppressed compromising information about President Donald Trump, a nearly equal-sized majority of Republicans are convinced there has been a coordinated effort by "unelected government officials" to undercut the Trump administration and alter the electoral vote in favor of President Biden.[3]

Pundits once spoke of conspiracy thinking in America today as coming from a minority of Americans, but according to a December 10, 2020 Quinnipiac poll, currently 77 percent of polled Republicans believe the 2020 presidential election was stolen due to widespread election fraud.[4] Pundits are now calling this mainstream belief "madness," something said to be "unprecedented" among Americans as a whole. Apparently, for many Americans, ideology has become more important than democracy, justice, truth, and public health. Why is this so, we wonder, and where does this "madness" come from?

On the one hand, one could consider such views merely as temporary, passing fads and trends associated with the Trump presidency. One could also argue that the Trump era pandered to corporate and individual selfishness. According to Jason Johnson, professor of politics and journalism at Morgan State University, Donald Trump was good for conservative Republicans. He gave them tax cuts, altered voting and environmental regulations, and gutted regulations that protected women and minorities. If one looks at the Trump presidency from a policy perspective, he wasted a great deal of money and messed with the budget, but for many Republicans, he delivered a great many changes, results, and outcomes that they always wanted, no matter how achieved. Secondary concerns, such as his attitudes, personal behavior, or language, became excusable in the minds of many, because what matters is ideology.

If the current distortion continues, not only in Donald Trump's mind but also in the thinking of millions of his devoted followers, including many elected officials tied to his coattails, what lies ahead is uncertainty for the democratic process and possibly violence and civil disruption; big lies always end in violence.[5] One thing is certain: Americans will remain polarized and divided. Extensive social change is coming in America—indeed, is already present—and a great many Americans will resist it at all costs, even succumbing to delusion, hysteria, and conspiracy nonsense if necessary.

3. Cox and Halpin, "Conspiracy theories."
4. Keating, "Quinnipiac Poll."
5. I wrote this statement in December 2020, during the final months of the Trump presidency. On January 6, 2021, mob violence broke out in Washington, D.C., spurred on by Donald Trump at his "Save America Rally"; details of this event are given at the end of this chapter.

Is there a solution to conspiracy lies? Yes, I believe there is, and it lies in truth telling. When we think about truth in this way, each of us hits a wall, for to whom do we go for truth? In the past, people in doubt were told to go to experts or to someone in authority. However, that is exactly what so many Trump followers have done, choosing his words, guidance, and directives as truthful and authoritative. However, such allegiance led them to a dark place. There is an answer to linear, one-dimensional thinking, but it can only be found by listening to multiple points of view, and not simply to one. Then, after hearing, pondering, and digesting all major sides of an issue, truth-seekers need guidance from history before deciding on the best path to follow. Above all, seekers of truth need always to keep an open mind, remaining humble and teachable while avoiding adherence to a personality cult, that is, to a charismatic leader who demands allegiance. All humans are flawed, and no single individual has the absolute truth. Although I deal with cultic thinking and allegiance to personality cults and cultic leaders in the next chapter, my advice to people following charismatic leaders is to remain guarded around such individuals, always valuing the opinion and views of those who challenge their behavior and beliefs. In this regard, I encourage truth-seekers to avoid depending on the same source for news and perspective. If we truly desire truth in our lives, it is important that we vary our television news networks, radio talk show hosts, online news sources, and other sources of information. Of course, there is nothing wrong with having favorite news programs, talk shows, or program hosts, but to rely only on one person or on one network for facts or truth can easily lead to error, falsehood, and deception. Above all, we must rely on news sources that are committed to accuracy and transparency.

Whenever multiple individuals in authority or with proven credentials question the views or behavior of a charismatic leader, particularly one who has alienated others through belligerence, derision, or disrespect, we have good reason to avoid such individuals and to question their views and beliefs. In addition, whenever someone claims an exclusive hold on the truth, we can be sure he or she cannot be trusted. This holds true in all fields of belief, be they philosophical, sociological, political, philosophical, and theological. Truth is not something that one individual or group, isolated from humanity as a whole, can be said to embody, for truth is not something individuals possess. Rather, truth is something that possesses those who are aligned with the whole of humanity and the whole of reality, a state of spirituality few of us attain. Those who reach such a stage of enlightenment, labeled "universalizing faith" by James Fowler, live their lives to the full in service of others without real worry or spiritual doubt. Truth, for such people, is not factual, cognitive, or sectarian but relational in nature and universal in scope.

To understand conspiracy thinking, psychologists examine personality types in search of explanations for susceptibility to misinformation and to outlandish beliefs. In so doing, specific personality profiles appear as distinct: (1) impulsive and overconfident personalities eager to espouse gullibility and naiveté in others, but not in themselves. (2) A second type is more solitary, moody, and anxious, including those who are detached, older, or living alone. According to a recent Emory University study, some personalities seem resistant to conspiracy theories (involving around 60 percent of individuals), while the remainder (some 40 percent) seem more susceptible.[6]

Of course, conspiracy theories are as old as human society, found in all times, places, and cultures around the globe. In times when communities were small and vulnerable, being on guard for hidden plots and threatening persons was likely a matter of personal survival. In addition to security, psychologists also find that people adopt conspiracy beliefs as a balm for deep grievance. Conspiracy theories provide a sense of control, an internal narrative to make sense of a world that seems senseless. The presence of a pandemic, such as happened in 2020 and 2021, creates a perfect storm for conspiracy theories and false beliefs, resulting in credible explanations for those with fears of getting sick and dying or of infecting others. Moreover, fear distracts people from judging the accuracy of reports they may hear or read.

In a September 28, 2020 article on conspiracy theories in the *New York Times*, Benedict Carey examined the results of a *Journal of Personality* study titled "Looking Under the Tinfoil Hat: Clarifying the Psychological and Psychopathological Correlates of Conspiracy Beliefs." According to authors Shauna M. Bowes and Scott O. Lilienfeld, the personality features that more solidly link to conspiracy beliefs include entitlement, self-centered impulsivity, cold-heartedness, elevated levels of depressive moods and anxiousness—including moods such as anger and frustration and tendencies such as narcissism—and a group of personality disorders called "psychoticism," a core feature of psychosis that characterizes schizophrenia. On the other hand, qualities such as sociability,

---

6. Naftulin, "Conspiracy theories."

conscientiousness, modesty, and altruism are seen to act as deterrents to conspiracy beliefs, although only slightly so. Surprisingly, levels of sincerity and self-esteem were found to bear no apparent relation to a person's susceptibility.

Such lack of precision regarding correlation between personality and conspiracy beliefs should come as no surprise, however. As Bowes indicates, in the case of belief systems, the results of personality tests are not always clear or convincing, "for personality tests are not very good measures of things we don't understand very well."[7]

Assault on the U.S. Capitol

On January 6, 2021, a day when the U.S. Congress convened to certify the Electoral College victory of Joseph Biden in the 2020 race for the White House, mob violence broke out in Washington, D.C. following a call to action by outgoing President Donald Trump to a massive crowd of followers gathered at his request. At the so-called "Save America" Rally, Trump, his sons, and Rudy Giuliani called thousands of loyal Trump supporters to pressure lawmakers to overturn the election results, declaring Trump winner. As a result, hundreds of insurrectionists, some having received insider help and information from disgruntled members of Congress, stormed the barricades surrounding the Capitol. Forcing their way into the halls of Congress, they threatened the lives of lawmakers assembled to certify the 2020 election. Many of these insurrectionists carried Confederate flags and U.S. flags with replicas of Trump's face engraved on them—a desecration of America and a subterfuge for a personality cult over true patriotism. Breaking doors and windows, they stormed Congress with impunity, members of security resisting bravely as scores of aggressive thugs roamed the halls of Congress. Armed with weapons and carrying zip-tie handcuffs, the ringleaders were intent on apprehending Vice President Mike Pence, with the intent of forcibly removing him from the Capitol and taking him to a makeshift gallows erected. Others sought House Speaker Nancy Pelosi, intent on killing her and any other so-called obstructionist lawmakers they might find. Vandalizing offices and desecrating symbols of authority, they forced lawmakers to evacuate the halls of Congress in search of safety. Later, live bombs were found to have been planted near political party offices. The event, soon dubbed

---

7. Bowes, cited in Carey, "Conspiracy Theories."

"America's second day of infamy," resulted in death and bloodshed. Only later, following initial confusion and administrative indecision, National Guard troops were deployed to restore order. Shortly thereafter, following resignations by Trump appointees (including members of his Cabinet), legislators and even some Trump loyalists began calling for the resignation or removal of President Trump from office. Eventually, Trump was impeached for having incited violence. The assault on the Capitol had become an assault against democracy.

After losing the election, Trump tried to overturn the results, first legally, through courts and election boards, and then illegally, by abusing his powers, pressuring legislators, then secretaries of state, even the Vice President of the United States, telling them to break election laws to give him a victory. Finally, when all else failed, the president and his team used intimidation to incite violence, which resulted in multiple injuries and five deaths. The results could have been worse, including the killing of Pence and congressional legislators, as crowd chants indicated. Up to that point, Pence had been Trump's most loyal backer. However, Trump showed he cared more about himself, worrying little if others or even if the law got in the way.

The following Sunday, during an interview by host Fareed Zakaria on the CNN Global Public Square show, retired general and former Secretary of State Colin Powell indicated that while national healing could not take place without legal accountability by those guilty of aiding and abetting the insurrection, this was a time for setting aside partisan politics and focusing on unity and citizenship. At this point, he pled, America needs neither Republicans or Democrats but American citizens who are willing to negotiate opposing points of view peacefully and respectfully. This is American democracy at its best, its greatest heritage.

Despite the mayhem of January 6, that evening the members of Congress reconvened to certify the election. Originally, some 140 representatives in the House and some 14 senators had declared their opposition to the democratic process that secured the election for President-elect Biden and Vice President-elect Kamala Harris. While some of these lawmakers changed their mind following the mob violence, the majority persisted in their belief that the election had been stolen, all based on lies and conspiracy theories. In protesting the election, some elected officials, like Ted Cruz and junior senator Josh Hawley of Missouri, put their political ambitions above their nation. At one point, Hawley fist saluted the crowd, exhorting the rebels with resolve. Demonstrating that even elected officials can be deceived, such men betrayed their oath to the Constitution, putting loyalty to flawed individuals above the nation, the constitution, and their oath of office. In normal times, the certification process would have been routine and the votes certified ceremoniously, in celebration of democracy. However, these are not normal times. As seems likely, more violence awaits, as calls go forth on the Internet for continued action across the nation. It may take years, even decades, for this rebellious threat to be eradicated.

Testing Our Beliefs

No person I know—certainly no adult—chooses to believe a lie. All of us want to believe what is true. Thus, I am surprised that, in the realm of religion, so many people are willing to base their lives upon untested and even highly disputed beliefs, beliefs most of them received as children. All authentic religions, like their philosophical, social, and political counterparts, seek to discover the truth underlying their values and assumptions. However, truth is not always verifiable, and not all beliefs are objectively true. It is our task, as informed human beings, to assess the veracity of our faith statements and beliefs. For those who are willing to test their beliefs, even to expose them to doubt, the truth will inevitably unfold with clarity and conviction, resulting in spiritual growth and transformation.

The 2021 assault on democracy underscored the power of rhetoric. Utilized by demagogues, autocrats, tyrants, and dictators in the past, the use of rhetoric in America as a vehicle for mass violence, unlawful action, and disbelief seemed impossible until then. However, civil discontent has simmered in the United States since the Civil War, the most recent flashpoint being the Obama presidency. Underlying all hate groups in America are racism and sexism, themselves a sign of widespread moral sickness. Surprisingly, this madness overtook many Republicans in 2020, loyal to a political party vastly different from what it had been even five years earlier. Instead of reflecting the image of Lincoln and Reagan, the Republican Party had been remade in the image of Trump, more a cult of personality than ever before. Despite hopeful signs of patriotism in the party, such as evident in the Lincoln Project, the Republican Accountability Project, and other groups and individuals within the Republican Party protecting American democracy, the party seems to have veered to the far right, in part as a response to extremism in the Democratic Party. While a two-party system is essential to American democracy, only a return to civility and moderation can fill the current vacuum at the middle of the American political spectrum. America needs moderates now more than ever. For Republicans, this means a return to "common-sense conservatism"; for Democrats, a return to "common-sense liberalism."

While Donald Trump can be blamed for inciting delusional ideology, his election only sparked the tinder already present, aided by a growing opposition to social, political, and economic changes enacted during the Obama presidency. While Trump's "Make America Great Again" ideology certainly involves racist, homophobic, and xenophobic tendencies, the widespread delusional susceptibility of many Americans to conspiracy thinking has, I believe, a religious element, broadly rooted in its faith dimension but also in specific beliefs associated with America's Christian heritage, particularly as expressed and understood by Christianity's conservative faith traditions. In my estimation, conservative religious mindsets inherently contain attitudes and outlooks suspicious and intolerant of alternative ideologies, cultures, beliefs, and behaviors, while remaining susceptible to extreme and even delusional aspects of their own religious beliefs and behavior.

As Robert P. Jones writes in *White Too Long: The Legacy of White Supremacy in American Christianity*, White American evangelicals are the biggest obstacle in the struggle for social equality and justice in the United States. Statistically they have proven to be less compassionate, empathetic, and hospitable to racial justice than other Americans, while also more hostile toward immigrants. Studies indicate that hyper conservative and reactionary ways of being Christian, that is, rationalistic, literalistic, and legalistic ways of living and thinking, contribute to racism, sexism, nationalism, exclusivism, and other harmful ideologies.

Raised as an evangelical Christian and speaking as a "progressive conservative," it is my hope that Christians of all stripes can join forces with people of all races, genders, and creeds to chart a more helpful and hopeful religious climate for our society, our nation, and our world. In the words of the Latin phrase *Juncta Juvant*, "together we thrive."

Questions for Discussion and Reflection

1. What is a conspiracy theory, and why are increasingly large numbers of Americans espousing conspiracy theories?
2. Do you question the reliability of mainstream media reporting in America? Explain your answer.
3. Do you agree with the author that truth telling is a solution to disinformation and conspiracy theories? Don't both sides on an issue—those who believe and those who disbelieve conspiracy theories—believe that truth is on their side? Is there a way around this impasse? If truth telling is based on "facts," are such facts inherently objective to those who sincerely seek the truth? Explain your answer.
4. Are you suspicious of people who claim an exclusive hold on the truth? Have you ever been misled or deceived by a person in authority? If so, what was its effect on you, and how did you respond?
5. In societal response to violent civil disobedience, such as the mob assault on the U.S. Capitol on January 6, 2021, what comes first, accountability (such as the prosecution of rioters) or national healing? In cases of national disunity and division, are these two responses harmonious or counterproductive?
6. In your estimation, does religion play a role in susceptibility to conspiracy thinking? Explain your answer.

Chapter 2

Dynamics of Cult Development

THE SECOND HALF OF the twentieth century witnessed the proliferation of cultic mindsets and movements in the United States. While the phenomenon of cultic sectarianism flourished during the nineteenth century in America, cultic movements and personalities increased during the 1960s and 1970s, spreading their mind-bending influence over vast segments of the American populace in the early decades of the twenty-first century. American susceptibility to deviant thought led to the widespread belief in lies, irrational beliefs, fake news, and conspiracy theories that divided America politically, socially, and religiously during the Obama and Trump presidencies (2008–2020) and beyond.

Why are millions of Americans today susceptible to disinformation? Surely one explanation is our reptilian brain (the instinctive brain present before birth), designed to protect us in the face of threat, real or perceived. Other explanations focus on personality traits and mental health. In this study, I wish to focus on another explanation, namely, the human religious impetus that flows from our innate spirituality, a corollary of the imagination that fuels our faith dimension. This dimension—influenced by our creativity and rationality but also by our emotional states, hopes, and fears—shapes the worldviews that guide our lives, perspectives grounded in theological, philosophical, and psychological considerations. From these perceptions flow ideologies, cults, sects, and eventually, organized religions. Other factors, psychological, social, and political, also lead to the explosion of delusional thinking and antisocial behavior evident in America today.

Dynamics of Cult Development

In the United States, cultic belief and behavior flourish due to five interrelated factors: (1) civil liberties, such as freedom of expression and belief, (2) a culture of permissiveness, (3) a questing spirit, energized by elements such as capitalism, scientific inquiry, entrepreneurship, and a belief in the inevitability of progress, (4) the separation of church and state, and (5) the notion of American democracy, understood as the ability of each individual to intuit what might be best for him or her. Recognizing the influence of these factors, this book focuses on the impact of the Christian ethos—its beliefs and practices—on the American mind.

The Cultic Mindset

While cults need not be religious in nature, experts generally agree on certain marks of cultic movements, including the following characteristics:

1. A charismatic leader. A cult is usually started by a dynamic individual with great personal magnetism, with a genius for attracting followers and inspiring their confidence. Cult leaders are generally self-centered and narcissistic, often promoting self-deification. As cult leaders gain followers, they and their members come to believe that they are the exclusive followers of God and hence, the one true church or cause.

2. Authoritarian structure. The pyramid authority structure—rule from the top down—is the pattern in most cults. The cult leader is revered and obeyed, and absolute submission to the leader and the hierarchy is required.

3. New revelation. This charismatic leader tends to be a strong personality who is unwilling to accept traditional teachings and so develops a peculiar set of beliefs, imbued with unique authority.

4. Total commitment. A cult has rigid standards for membership and accepts no members who will not become fully committed to the group. Loyalty and obedience are crucial. In some cases, followers are admonished to "forsake all other views" and even to turn over all personal property to the organization. Members of the group acquire a we/they mindset, in which they are right and all others are wrong. Hence, members are prone to suspicion, delusion, and conspiracy thinking.

5. Intensive indoctrination. All cults subject new converts to intensive indoctrination. During the indoctrination period, there is constant supervision. Members are given little time to think or sleep. Many ex-members testify to having been hypnotized or brainwashed by this high-pressure indoctrination.

6. Persecution complex. Cult leaders generally are paranoid, viewing "outsiders" with suspicion and antagonism, including the press and parents seeking to retrieve their children. Paranoia extends to those inside as well as outside the organization. If there is any doubt or question of the group and its beliefs, its source must be satanic or demonic.

7. Zealous proselytism. Members of cults spend a great deal of time proselytizing potential converts and demonizing opponents or opposing viewpoints.

8. "Last days" belief. Many modern cults teach that we are living in the last days—the end time of civilization. Temporal concerns are less important than adhering to the truth propagated by the group. Only the group's members will be spared impending doom and participate in the benefits of the world to come.

When I started this book, writing a chapter on cultic beliefs and behavior seemed obvious. Having studied Christianity-based cults in college with Walter Martin, then the leading evangelical expert on the topic of cults in America, I learned to distinguish the biblical worldview from the ideologies of cultic movements.

In the 1960s and 1970s, when I completed my formal education, Western cultic groups such as The Way International, The Children of God, and Erhard Seminar Training (known as est), and Eastern cultic movements such as the Hare Krishnas and Maharishi Mahesh Yogi's Transcendental Meditation flourished in the United States. Walter Martin and other evangelical Christian scholars with whom I studied often included Mormonism, Christian Science, Jehovah's Witnesses, and Seventh-Day Adventism among the cults, though this form of labeling, viewed as pejorative, gradually grew out of favor with more ecumenically minded Christians. Eventually, my focus on biblical studies, world religion, and the history of Christianity, aided by progressive and inclusive thinking, led me away from the topic of the cults, and I set aside my interest in cultic practice and belief.

Scholars in the field of Christianity-based cults generally define a "cult" as a minority religious group holding beliefs regarded as unorthodox or spurious, assessing such groups not only for their exclusive beliefs, but also for their manipulative mindset. Of course, such labeling is suspect, for it is used widely of outsiders and by members of one religious group against another. Religious cults, by definition, believe they alone have the truth, but on one level, this could be said historically of every religious movement, particularly in its formative stage. Ever since the Reformation, Catholics have labeled Protestants cultists or heretical, and Protestants have been all too happy to return the favor. The important thing to realize is that cultic belief and behavior are part of every religion, and quite possibly even a phase in faith formation.

While many cults vanish with the death of their founders, cultic personalities and cultic mindsets continue. Some observers label cultic the autocratic behavior of President Trump during his presidency, both in his susceptibility to delusional thinking and in his obsessive need for loyalty from his followers and advisors. In *The Dangerous Case of Donald Trump*, thirty-seven psychiatrists and mental health experts assess former President Trump's mental state, pronouncing him psychopathic and dangerous. Like many cult leaders, he is declared narcissistic and delusional, caring only about himself. Unable to love others, he is quick to turn on those who show the slightest sign of disloyalty, including his most loyal followers. Even his final Twitter message on January 6, 2021 to insurrectionists who stormed the Capitol, "We love you," is an example of the rhetoric used by cultic leaders when recruiting newcomers, a technique called "love bombing."

Don't Drink the Kool-Aid

Some cultic beliefs are dangerous and reprehensible, a threat to the well-being of their followers. Perhaps the most notorious case is that of Peoples Temple leader Jim Jones, who on November 18, 1978 instructed all members living in the Jonestown compound in Guyana to commit an act of "revolutionary suicide" by drinking poisoned punch. In all, 918 people died that day, nearly a third of whom were children. The Jonestown Massacre was the most deadly single non-natural disaster in U.S. history until September 11, 2001. The Jonestown Massacre also remains the only time in history in which a U.S. congressman (Leo Ryan) was killed in the line of duty.

Founded in 1956 by Rev. Jim Jones, the Peoples Temple began as a racially integrated church that focused on helping people in need. Jones originally established the Peoples Temple in Indianapolis, Indiana, but then moved it to Redwood Valley, California in 1966. Jones had a vision of a utopian community in which everyone lived together in harmony and worked for the common good. The movement prospered in California, but Jones yearned to establish a compound outside of the United States, where he could maintain full control, far from interference by the U.S. government. In 1973, he leased land from the Guyanese government and had workers clear it of jungle. In early 1977, about fifty people lived in the compound. Jones remained in the U.S. until he received word that an exposé was about to be printed about him, featuring interviews by ex-members. Jones immediately left for Guyana, accompanied by several hundred Peoples Temple members.

Life in Jonestown was not ideal. In conditions of high heat and humidity, members were put to work, often up to eleven hours a day. Throughout the compound, members could hear Jones's voice broadcast through a loudspeaker. While some members loved living there, others wished to leave. However, the compound was surrounded by miles of jungle and encircled by armed guards. By this time, Jones was fully delusional, claiming to be the reincarnation of Jesus Christ and demanding God-like devotion and obedience.

When Representative Leo Ryan of California heard negative reports, he decided to go to Jonestown to investigate, taking with him an NBC film crew and a group of concerned relatives of Peoples Temple members. At first things went well, but soon some members passed a note to one of the film's crewmembers, inscribed with the names of people who wanted to leave. The following day, November 18, Ryan announced that he was willing to take anyone who wished to leave back to the United States. Worried about Jones's reaction, only a few people accepted the offer.

During their departure, Ryan was attacked by a Peoples Temple member. Aware that he and the others were in danger, Ryan boarded a truck and left the compound. The truck made it safely to the airport, but the planes weren't ready to leave when the group arrived. As they waited, a tractor and trailer pulled up near them. From the trailer, Peoples Temple members emerged and started shooting at Ryan's group. On the tarmac, five people were killed, including Congressman Ryan.

Back in Jonestown, Jones ordered everyone to gather at the pavilion. Once everyone had assembled, Jones spoke to his congregation. He was in a panic and seemed agitated. He was upset that some of his members had left. He told the congregation that there had been an attack on Ryan's group. He also told them that because of the attack, Jonestown wasn't safe. Jones was sure that the U.S. government would react strongly to the attack on Ryan's group.

Jones told his congregation that the only way out was to follow his orders, which included imbibing a prepared drink. They had been tested in this manner before, and the drink had been safe. But this time there was concern, for Jones spoke of the "revolutionary act" of suicide. One woman spoke up against the idea, but after Jones offered reasons why there was no hope in other options, the crowd spoke out against her. When it was announced that Ryan was dead, Jones became more urgent and more heated. Jones urged the congregation to commit suicide by saying, "If these people land out here, they'll torture some of our children here. They'll torture our people, they'll torture our seniors. We cannot have this." Large kettles filled with grape-flavored Flavor-Aid (not Kool-Aid), cyanide, and Valium were placed in the open-sided pavilion. Babies and children were brought up first. Syringes were used to pour the poisoned juice into their mouths. Mothers then drank some of the poisoned punch. Oher members followed. Some members were already dead before others got their drinks. If anyone wasn't cooperative, there were guards with guns and crossbows to encourage them. It took approximately five minutes for each person to die.

A sealed note found on the cult commander's body, written by a desperate follower just prior to the ritual suicide, underscored the despair and isolationism of cultists. "Dad," the note said, "I see no way out. I agree with your decision—I fear only that without you the world may not make it." On that day, 912 people died from drinking the poison, 276 of whom were children. Jones died from a single gunshot wound to the head, but it is unclear whether he did this himself. Only a handful of people survived, either by escaping into the jungle or hiding somewhere in the compound. In total 918 people died, either at the airport or at the Jonestown compound.

The Outsider Test for Faith

I am a fan of the Outsider Test for Faith, formulated by former evangelical John W. Loftus. This approach encourages individuals of various faiths to assess their truth claims from the perspective of an outsider and with the same level of skepticism they use to evaluate other religious traditions. As the Outsider Test for Faith makes clear, no one religion can lay claim to ultimate truth, though most do so with regularity, particularly when challenged by competing perspectives. In the absence of an absolute, objective vantage point whereby all religious truths can be judged, it seems best to acknowledge that none has more than a temporal or subjective value.

When it comes to belief in miracles, it becomes obvious that while people can easily justify whatever they are raised to believe, they can just as easily dismiss what people in other religious traditions believe. Even today, many Christians reject miracle accounts in other religions, such as miracles in the Hindu tradition or, closer to home, those attributed to Joseph Smith, the founder of Mormonism, while not questioning miracles in their own tradition or those found in their scriptures. This inconsistency is not justifiable, unless one postulates that the laws of the universe are bent toward adherents of one's own faith or denomination.

When it comes to religious insiders, these are notoriously incapable of presenting factual evidence for their beliefs. Take for example *The Book of Mormon*, first published in 1830. All copies of that Mormon scripture include in the preface a statement known as "The Testimony of Three (later Eight) Witnesses" in the preface. These witnesses assisted Joseph Smith in the process of translating ancient golden plates into Mormon scripture, plates supposedly buried around 385 CE in upstate New York by Moroni, son of Mormon. Mormon, a military chief, was a Native American said to have descended from ancient Israelite tribes who migrated from the Middle East to America centuries before the time of Jesus. The ancient tablets, written in "Reformed hieroglyphics," were then "found" by Smith and translated into modern (King James) English with the aid of two spectacle stones, said to be the Urim and Thummim used by Israelite high priests in biblical times (see Ex 28:30; Lev 8:8; Deut 33:8).

Martin Harris, a wealthy farmer, began to assist Joseph Smith in the process of translation. During the translation, Smith and the plates remained behind a curtain, with Harris on the other side taking dictation.

Dynamics of Cult Development

Eventually Oliver Cowdery, Smith's cousin, assisted as well. In the course of translating the plates, the text revealed that the plates were to be shown to others (see 2 Nephi 27:12–13), a select group that came to include David Whitmer. However, the three original "witnesses" to the process of translation were all later rejected by Mormons. Whitmer and Cowdery were charged as thieves and counterfeits, and Harris later changed his testimony to say that he only saw the plates with "the eyes of faith."[1] While Cowdery and Harris were eventually rebaptized, we can only wonder how much weight can be attached to a testimony coming from individuals of this sort. In addition, we all want to know what happened to the plates. Why are they no longer available? According to Mormon teaching, they were taken away by Moroni, now an angel, and hidden for all time. How convenient!

Shortly after 1830, a man named Solomon Spaulding, a retired minister living in Amity, Pennsylvania, some forty miles south of Pittsburgh, submitted a lawsuit claiming to be the author of the falsely published *Book of Mormon*. In his lawsuit, Spaulding claimed to have delivered a manuscript about the origin of the American Indians to a publisher in Pittsburgh some years earlier, a manuscript since lost by the publisher. Because there were no other copies of the manuscript, Spaulding could not prove his accusation, but due to his knowledge and interest in the topic of American Indians, he went on to write other novels on the subject.[2]

Coincidentally, while Smith was "translating" *The Book of Mormon*, he was living at the home of his father-in-law in Harmony, Pennsylvania, just north of Pittsburgh. At that time he became acquainted with Sidney Rigdon, a convert to Mormonism, who had a close friend who worked at the printing shop where Spaulding's manuscript went missing. Friends of Rigdon are on record stating that he showed them a novel portraying the biblical origin of American Indians. Rigdon was eventually accused of apostasy and excommunicated from the Mormon Church.

Mormon scholars have an explanation that disputes each of these claims, much like devout Christian theologians argue persuasively in favor of the validity and facticity of Christian dogmas and beliefs. In the realm of faith, all argumentation begins with presuppositions. Once initial premises are accepted as factual, most any conclusion is possible. This holds true for delusional beliefs as well. It is natural for Christian

---

1. Hoekema, *Four Major Cults*, 12–13.
2. Martin, *Kingdom of the Cults*, 223–26.

apologists to find "evidence" for Christian beliefs, as it is for outsiders to question and invalidate non-Christian religious claims and beliefs. What happens, however, when Christians apply the Outsider Test to their own faith assumptions? This is the question we ask and attempt to answer in this study.

Questions for Discussion and Reflection

1. What are the distinguishing marks of a cultic movement?
2. Have you ever had an encounter with someone from a religious cult? If so, describe your experience. If possible, describe the mindset or belief system of that individual or group.
3. Do you agree with those who label as cultic Christianity-based groups such as the Mormons or Jehovah's Witnesses? Explain your answer.
4. Can you provide examples of clergy, church workers, or church members who display cultic beliefs or behavior? Explain your answer.
5. In your own words, explain John Loftus's Outsider Test for Faith and assess its value.

Chapter 3

Dynamics of Faith Development

HISTORY REVEALS MANY INSTANCES when people submit to authoritarian rule, forcibly or willingly. Despite its pervasiveness, submission to cultic personalities and to other hierarchical patterns of control is counterintuitive to human growth and wellbeing. Cultic movements prevent people from growing emotionally, mentally, and spiritually, keeping them in a state of dependence and subservience. Control might be necessary for rebellious children and deviant adults, but it is unnatural to normal human development. As humans grow by progressing physically, psychologically, emotionally, and intellectually, so they undergo various stages of growth in their faith.

There is in every human an impetus which, when nourished, seeks health and wholeness. Healthy human beings are said to go through discernible stages of growth throughout their lifetime. According to psychologist Erik Erikson, psychosocial development proceeds by critical steps. Each stage is marked by crisis, connoting not a catastrophe but a turning point, a crucial period of increased vulnerability and heightened potential. At such points, achievements are won or failures occur, leaving the future to some degree better or worse but in any case, restructured.

Out of one's individuality flows a spirituality that also yearns for growth and expression. What Erikson contributed to our understanding of the stages of psychosocial development, Jean Piaget to the stages of cognitive development, and Lawrence Kohlberg to the stages of moral development, so James Fowler did for spirituality. He identified seven stages of faith, from stage zero, called "primal faith," when infants and toddlers develop (or fail to develop) a sense of safety about the universe and the divine, to a sixth stage called "universalizing faith." This level, rarely reached, characterizes those who live their lives to the full in service of others without any real fears or worries. Most people plateau at what Fowler calls the "synthetic-conventional" stage, one arising in adolescence. At this stage, authority is usually placed in individuals or groups that represent one's beliefs.[1]

If it takes a village to raise a child, it takes a lifetime to internalize and establish that child's total identity matrix. Just as cultural and racial identity unfolds over one's lifespan, so do gender, sexual, and religious identities, to name a few. Unraveling and reweaving the identity strands of one's experience is a never-ending task in a society where important dimensions of our lives are shaped by the simultaneous forces of progress and change. While it is true that simple dimensions of a person's complex, layered identity are often isolated and determined at an early age, for purposes of revitalization and transformation, the work of internalization does not stop with the resolution of conflicts surrounding one's identity. We humans continue to be works of progress for a lifetime.

What holds true for individuals applies to institutions as well. As societies grow, develop, and change, so also religions evolve, adapt, and change. Institutions that remain the same may appear solid, reliable, and true, but such perceptions are illusory and false. That which does not grow, dies, and that which does not adapt, becomes irrelevant. This principle encourages us to remain open to newness and change, individually, organizationally, and as a society.

Four Stages of Faith Development

In the late stages of the Trump presidency, my mind filled with cultic leaders, followers, and the cultic mindset, I noticed a publication announcement for Brian McLaren's newest book, *Faith After Doubt*. Inspired by the title, and familiar with McLaren books such as *A New Kind of Christian* trilogy, *A Generous Orthodoxy*, and *Naked Spirituality*, I ordered a copy, never imagining that it would serve as a template for this chapter. In that book, written mostly from personal experience, McLaren reveals aspects of his journey of faith, proposing "a model of faith development in which questions and doubt are not the enemy of faith but rather a portal to a more mature and fruitful kind of faith." That statement, taken from the

---

1. Fowler, *Stages of Faith*.

book's jacket cover, serves as an introduction to the stages of faith I lay out in this chapter.[2]

Despite including a fourth stage, these stages are similar to other models of faith development I have followed in previous writings, such as the precritical, critical, and postcritical model based on Paul Ricoeur's first and second naiveté; Richard Rohr's first and second half of life or his Order, Disorder, Reorder paradigm; and Søren Kierkegaard's aesthetic, ethical, and religious stages. While McLaren's model correlates with these and other stage theories of development, I find his four-stage approach best describes the faith journey for people reared in traditional forms of Christianity.

Doubt, it turns out, is the passageway from one stage to the next. Without doubt, there can be growth within a stage, but growth from one stage to another usually requires us to doubt the assumptions that give shape to our current stage. We will call the first period of growth Stage One, and the next period Stage Two, and so on. Each new stage, like a ring on a tree, embraces and builds upon the previous stage, while growing beyond its limits. Alternatively, to borrow a phrase from Ken Wilber, each stage includes and transcends its predecessors. McLaren labels the four stages: Simplicity, Complexity, Perplexity, and Harmony (which I call Clarity).

As it turns out, McLaren developed this framework earlier, having introduced it ten years earlier in *Naked Spirituality*, where he compared his stages to the four sequential seasons of spring, summer, fall, and winter, likening Simplicity to the springlike season of spiritual awakening, Complexity to the summerlike season of spiritual strengthening, Perplexity to the autumnlike season of spiritual surviving, and Harmony to the winterlike season of spiritual discovery.[3] Like living with nature, the point is not to stay in spring or summer forever, nor is it the point to get to (or through) winter as soon as possible, any more than the point of life is advancing from infancy to old age as soon as possible. Rather, the point is to live each stage fully, to learn well what each day and season has to teach, and to live and enjoy life in companionship with God and others through all of life's seasons.

In Stage One (Simplicity), which begins around the age of two, infants become increasingly independent, and it is the parents' task to

---

2. This segment is a summary and adaptation of McLaren, *Faith After Doubt*, 41–115.
3. McLaren, *Naked Spirituality*, 26–27.

teach them how to provide for their own needs and desires in appropriate ways. This stage revolves around the simple mental function of sorting nearly everything into one of two categories (things are either permitted or prohibited, others are either friend or foe, and one is either happy or sad). For that reason, in Stage One, you set out to master the mental skills of dualism, of seeing the world in twos (this or that, in or out, right or wrong).

Authorities—your parents, grandparents, teachers, political and religious leaders—are central to this stage; hence, Stage One is the stage of authority as well as the stage of dualism. As far as you are concerned, the authorities know everything, and you don't, so you feel highly dependent on them. You trust them and want to please them, and you aspire someday to be as certain and all-knowing as they are. Before long, you find out that the authorities in your life dislike or distrust other authorities, and your dualism adds a new category: us versus them. This social dualism creates a strong sense of loyalty and identity among "us." It also creates a strong sense of anxiety and even hostility about "them," the "other," the "outsider," and the "outcasts." Stage One is built on trust, because for the child, trust is an absolute necessity, a matter of survival. Simple trust, unquestioning loyalty, that's what matters in Stage One.

Stage One is the baseline of what being raised means in our culture. Here one is taught the difference between right and wrong and other basic dualisms of Stage One. While this stage works well from the age of two to twelve, many people spend their entire lives in Stage One, submitting to authorities and following all the rules. Then, when it is time for them to become authorities themselves, they demand the same submission from the next generation that they themselves gave to the previous generation. For that reason, it shouldn't be a surprise that faith and religion are a strictly Stage One phenomenon for millions, even billions, of people.

Thus far, Stage One may have felt like a school to help us learn the basic morals necessary for independence. However, at some point, it begins to feel like detention, even a prison. The only way out is doubt. We may doubt that the authorities are always right. We may doubt that all the rules are always absolute and appropriate. Add hormones, puberty, sexual curiosity, and changing brains to the mix, and Simplicity stops feeling appropriate anymore. This may happen at twelve or twenty-two or forty five, but eventually, many of us doubt our way out of Simplicity and enter Stage Two (Complexity).

If Stage One is about dualism and dependence, Stage Two is about pragmatism and independence. We have our own lives to live, and we have to find a way to become who we are on our own. In Stage One we were drawn to authority figures who told us what to think and do, but in Stage Two we seek out coaches who teach us how to think for ourselves and help us develop our own goals, along with out own skills to attain those goals. In Stage One, we saw life as a matter of survival, but in Stage Two we see life as a game, as a contest of competing and winning. In Stage Two everything is either known or knowable, but in Stage One, everything is learnable and doable, if only we can find the right models, mentors, and coaches, and master the right techniques, skills, and know-how.

In terms of our faith, we are no longer content merely to listen to a sermon by an authority figure; we want to learn methods of studying the Bible for ourselves. Learning and studying, thinking for ourselves and reaching our own conclusions, are part of what it means to be a good Stage Two Christian. People in Simplicity and Complexity become active consumers in the religious market. Every year, they need more sermons, books, radio and TV shows, podcasts, conferences, courses, retreats, camps, churches, and mission trips. For some people, the only faith they will ever know is either the authoritarian, dualistic faith of Stage One, or the pragmatic independent faith of Stage Two. However, what happens if you start to question your religious goals?

When people run into problems with Stage One or Two Christianity, many make a lateral transfer. They move from a Stage One Catholic to a Stage One Pentecostal, or from a Stage Two Presbyterian to a Stage Two Methodist. Some people make forward rather than lateral transfers. So a Stage One Catholic becomes a Stage Two Methodist or even a Buddhist. It feels like a step up, because developmentally, at least it is. Other disillusioned Stage Two Christians may temporarily or permanently revert to Stage One Christianity, making a regressive transfer. Sadly, a regressive transfer often leads the spiritually troubled into cults or cult like groups, which are fiercely devoted to rigid Simplicity. For those who regress, the fear of what lies beyond Complexity feels so terrifying, or the sense of belonging that is often found in strict Stage One communities feels so alluring, that they willingly resubmit to Stage One authority, or even to authoritarianism. With regards to reading the Bible, they willingly revert to literalism.

When Stage Two people find religious teaching or programming doesn't produce the results they expected, many sincere believers simply amp up their effort, assuming the fault is their own. But eventually their confidence cracks, doubts pour in, and their Stage Two project starts to sink. For most Stage Two believers, however, there is no going back, at least not in the long term. That's when some people go from precritical to critical thinking and living. Having felt increasingly alienated from Stage One dualism and Stage Two pragmatism, they lose faith in both the authoritarian leaders of Simplicity and the success coaches of Complexity, whether inside or outside the church. Both types of leaders make promises they cannot deliver, and neither type is honestly facing life's deeper questions and challenges.

After trying lateral transfers among two or more Stage Two faith communities, some start doubting the whole faith project. They begin to feel so stuck, trapped, and stagnant they decide to burn down the whole structure. On their way out of the burning building, many grab for mementos of the faith to save. Others barely make it out alive, saving nothing but their lives.

Other people aren't so easily satisfied. Their quest for honesty and depth burns like a fire in the belly and they move into Stage Three (Perplexity). Life for people in Stage Three feels more than simple and more than complex; it is simultaneously perplexing and mysterious. What physicists say about quantum mechanics becomes true for all of life: reality is not only stranger than we imagine, but stranger that we can imagine. Appearances deceive; full truths become less convenient than half-truths and lies.

Stage Three is not amenable to stable, long-lasting congregations. Stage Three communities tend to self-destruct in various ways. Stage Three people, for example, see the damage done by unchallenged structures and institution, so they distrust and challenge even their own institutions. In contrast to Stage One people, who are dependent on authority figures, and in contrast to Stage Two people, who seek coaches who will help them in their quest to be independent, Stage Three people tend to be counter-dependent. As a result, they tend to use, exhaust, and discard their leaders quickly. Furthermore, because this stage embraces relativism, Stage Three people feel more comfortable lurking on the fringes of a group rather than belonging squarely in its center. Even better, they might be fringe members of a number of groups, to gain a variety of viewpoints. Unable to find a community that fits their stage, many become unaffiliated "nones," walking out their questions alone. If they find community at all, it tends to be among alienated individuals like themselves.

Stage Three, even though it brings new gains, with multiple highs and thrills, often feels conflicted and heavy, like a feeling of descent and loss. Stage Two built so naturally on Stage One, and even the portal of doubt between the two was a relatively easy passage compared to Stage Three. Now, however, everything we once constructed we now deconstruct. The summits we climbed in Stage Two we now leave behind. Will anything remain, or will we end up in a state of spiritual bankruptcy?

Over time, we come to see that our grim "all is lost" assessment isn't the whole story. For example, in Stage Three, we still retain powerful and valuable treasures that we gained in Stage One. We learned, through dualism, to care about whether we are doing right or wrong. We learned to tell the truth. We learned to stand for something. Now, in Stage Three, our courageous commitment to honesty in the face of great cost and loss shows how well we learned the moral lessons of Simplicity. Similarly, in Stage Three we retain powerful treasures that we gained in Stage Two. We learn to be curious and flexible. We learn that different spheres of life are like games that operate by different sets of rules, and we become fluent in the complex rules of multiple games. We learn independence, and become self-motivated learners and self-managers, adults who begin to take responsibility for our own successes and failures.

Thus, despite the feelings of loss, the lasting gains of Stages One and Two sustain us in Perplexity. In addition, Stage Three will do the same for Stage Four. The fact is, Perplexity brings some of the greatest spiritual gifts life has to offer, gifts such as humility, honesty, courage, and sensitivity, for it is the doorstep to Stage Four, whether it be called the postcritical phase, the second simplicity, Clarity, or Harmony.

Whereas Perplexity is a path of descent, it is also a path of dissent. It gives us the courage to speak our truth, even when we are threatened for doing so. That courage is not simply an intellectual matter; it is also ethical, a matter of integrity and character. It may begin with doubt in ideas and beliefs, such as whether the earth was created in six literal days, whether evolution is a hoax, the Bible God's inerrant textbook full of history and scientific facts, or whether God destines human souls for heaven or for hell. Then it may doubt the authority figures who defend these beliefs, people whose motives, we come to understand, are often more about money, power, and privilege than about faith, hope, love, and service. Finally, we might question the superiority of Christianity over other religions, or the system of white supremacist Christianity in America that justified land theft, genocide, slavery, and apartheid, or the system of the

Religious Right that strained out gnats but eventually swallowed Donald Trump whole.

Perplexity, while it is deconstructive, is not meant to be destructive. Even though it questions and challenges conventional thinking, it is not immoral. It is a constructive stage of dissent on its way toward love. Even though people in Simplicity and Complexity see dissent as a danger to avoid, the world would be ethically impoverished if conventional notions of purity, loyalty, authority, and liberty went unchallenged. In this way, Stage Three dissenters, by questioning and challenging beliefs, norms, authority figures, and systems that are harming people, help everyone, including those in Stages One and Two who don't approve of their dissent.

If Stage Three dissenters keep descending through Perplexity, they will encounter a moment of crisis. Will their power of critical thinking become a gift that undoes them, or will the seeing through of skeptical doubt lead them into mystical or contemplative insight? Will they see through and beyond Simplicity, Complexity, and Perplexity to a deeper narrative, a more mysterious coherence, a revolutionary Harmony that embraces and integrates all it includes, producing a way to see things whole again?

People deep in Perplexity, feeling disillusioned with naïve dualism and pragmatism, face a stark choice. Will they become cynical nihilists, seeing everything so critically that meaning, purpose, value, reverence, and wonder become increasingly distant and elusive? For some people, this cynicism is the only intellectually honest option, so they surrender to perpetual Perplexity, all dressed up in critical thinking with nowhere to go. Nevertheless, some people can't be satisfied with that choice. They become cynical of their own cynicism, skeptical of their own skepticism, critical of their own critical thinking, even doubting their doubtfulness. They begin to wonder, hope, and imagine, and they dare to believe that there is another option beyond Stage Three. To maintain momentum, to keep growing and developing, however, requires a kind of dying, a death to ego or pride, a relinquishment of our right to judge, to know, and to control. You might call this a death to privilege, superiority, or supremacy, as seekers realize that all people share in the human condition.

At some point, this discovery of unifying Harmony beyond disintegrating Perplexity seems very simple, almost childish, like a return home. Perhaps this is what T. S. Eliot had in mind when he wrote, "We shall not cease from exploring, and the end of our exploring will be to arrive where we started and know the place for the first time." For this reason, Clarity has been described as a second naiveté, a second simplicity or innocence, "where instead of seeing through everything, we see into everything, and at the core, we find not meaninglessness and banality but profound, inexpressible belovedness and beauty."[4] This expansion can best be described as transcendence, a transcendence, however, that combines the best of the conservative and the best of the progressive positions, because it brings along or includes the previous stages rather than leaving them behind.

Stage Four (Clarity) builds on "the still more excellent way of love" described by Paul in his letter to the Corinthians (1 Cor 12:31–14:1). In this passage, Paul makes clear that nearly everything religious people strive for will eventually be embraced by something deeper. Even faith and hope don't have the last word. Only love, he says, is the more excellent way. In his masterpiece *The Brothers Karamazov*, Dostoyevsky captured this shift to Clarity when he admonished his readers to "Love all God's creation, the whole and every grain of sand in it. Love every leaf, every ray of God's light. Love the animals, love the plants, love everything. If you love everything, you will perceive the divine mystery in things. Once you perceive it, you will begin to comprehend it better every day. And you will come at last to love the whole world with an all-embracing love."

If in Stage One we know that everything is knowable, in Stage Two we know that everything is doable, and in Stage Three we know that everything is relative, in Stage Four we come to know that everything is suitable for its time (Eccl 3:11). In this stage we can finally accept that all our knowing, past and present, is partial (1 Cor 13:12). Now we finally see authority figures neither as omniscient and trustworthy (as in Stages One and Two) nor as fake or deluded (as in Stage Three), but rather as human beings like us, mortal and fallible. This awareness also allows us to find our identity in new ways in relation to others; not in Stage One dependence, nor in Stage Two independence, and not in Stage Three counterdependence, but in the more mature interdependence of nonduality. This humility before others morphs into what some call paradoxy—the realization that no statement about God—or even about what is true—can be final or complete.

This new realization—likened to a second Simplicity—eventually matures into a higher Complexity, and so on, in an ascending spiral of growth and discovery that continues as long as life itself. Far from feeling

---

4. McLaren, *Faith After Doubt*, 97.

we have finally arrived, in Stage Four we finally begin to understand that arrival has never been the goal.

In Stage Four we discover amazing truths. For example, we discover that spirituality is about love; that knowing is loving; that we know ourselves by loving ourselves; that we know others by loving them; that we know God by loving ourselves and others. When all is said and done, love is the answer, because love has the final say. Love is life's first experience, and it is life's final experience. For this we were born; for this we live; for this we die. To paraphrase the Greek philosopher Epimenides, cited by Paul in Acts 17:28, "In love we live and move and have our being."

Those who reach Stage Four do not experience Certainty, however, for that is the concern of those in Stages One and Two. Stage Four people never feel they have arrived. They are not obsessed with misguided notions of certainty or supremacy—more the opposite. Committed to the faith journey, they know there is no such thing as certainty in faith. Faith, like all creativity, flourishes not in certainty but in questioning, not in security but in venturing. In Stage Four, it is trust that matters, and qualities such as peace, harmony, joy, relationships, intimacy, and unity.

Those who reach Stage Four can look back and see that each stage contributed to Clarity. No stage was bad because it wasn't Stage Four (that would be a Stage One thing to say). Neither was any stage a distraction, delay, or obstacle to success because it wasn't Stage Four (that would be a Stage Two thing to say). Nor was any stage futile and in vain because it wasn't as mature and complete as Stage Four (that would be a Stage Three thing to say). Rather, each stage makes a vital contribution, appropriate for a time, which makes possible what follows, and each stage remains a central element of what follows. No stage is the destination, for each plays a vital role in the journey toward and into Harmony, toward nondiscriminatory, revolutionary love.

Those who reach Stage Four can also look back and see love's gravitational pull all along. When they loved correctness in Stage One, the love with which they pursued correctness mattered more. When they loved effectiveness in Stage Two, the love that moved them to pursue effectiveness mattered still more. When they loved honesty and justice in Stage Three, honesty and love mattered, but the love that burned in their heart for them mattered still more. Faith was about love all alone. They just didn't realize it, and it took doubt to help them see it.

As we conclude this chapter, we must acknowledge that this talk of stages, while arbitrary and imprecise, is a way to acknowledge the messiness of life. The journey of faith is not a neat progression, and the lines between stages are certainly arbitrary. Are there two stages, three, four, or more? Perhaps we might say there are twelve stages, since each of the four stages has an early period and a late period, with a section in between. Not only that, but we often find ourselves straddling stages, even functioning at different stages simultaneously, differently at school, work, home, or in church. The fact is, there is no more of a clear line between stages than there is a clear line between seasons. You can have warm days in winter and snowfall in spring, and just as calendars don't tell the whole story, neither can any schema. There is no shame, pride, or regret in being at the stage of development in which we find ourselves. If there is anything to regret, I suppose it is refusing to grow when life invites us to do so, or rushing through our current stage without learning all it has to teach us.

In whatever stage we find ourselves, particularly those of us who identify with a specific religious tradition, we can be sure that the most vocal and assertive members of our tradition rarely speak from a place of Harmony. They might be intensely committed, passionately loyal, and highly confident, but when these passionate spokespeople attack people of other religions, or use stereotypes and dehumanizing language that pave the way for suspicion, hostility, and violence, they are doing so out of fear and insecurity, not out of love. Very often, these spokespeople function as gatekeepers who target even more viciously members of their own sect or religion who express doubt about group norms. Gatekeepers typically label doubters as liberal, apostate, heretical, infidel, unwelcome, and dangerous. Such thinking and stereotyping is what I call Cultic Christianity.

The reverse is true of those in Stage Four, for they appreciate diverse viewpoints and genuinely love people from other faiths and traditions. Interestingly, entry into Stage Four faith doesn't make one less wholeheartedly Christian, Muslim, Buddhist, or Jewish, but more.

Questions for Discussion and Reflection

1. Assess the usefulness of the four-stage model of faith development presented in this chapter.
2. In which phase or stage of faith do you currently find yourself? Explain your answer.

3. Do you believe it is possible to be in more than one stage of faith simultaneously, or to be able to move backward as well as forward along the faith spectrum? Explain your answer.

4. If you ever found yourself in the spiritual stage of Perplexity, were you able to move forward to Stage Four? If so, how did this change occur? If not, why not?

5. Do you believe, with the apostle Paul, that "love is the answer" to life's challenges and perplexities, or does the word "love" sound too naïve, simplistic, or sentimental? Explain your answer.

6. What holds true for individuals also applies to institutions. If you are a member of a church or other religious organization, does it appear to be focused on only one stage of faith, or does it adequately provide for the needs of members in more than one stage? Explain your answer.

Chapter 4

Rethinking the Role of Religion

THE ROLE OF RELIGION, whether in formulating a worldview or in shaping a lifestyle, has until recently been considered indispensable. Religion is one of several systems devised by humans to provide guidance and meaning to the whole order of existence. The original role of religion was not divisive but holistic. It was not about creating polarities, institutions, hierarchies, or doctrines. Rather, the original role of religion was to promote harmonious spirituality.

The phenomenon of religion has been pervasive throughout the history of humanity and continues to be central to most cultures of the world. The role of religion in the current clash between cultures, whether viewed through a secular, traditional, or fundamentalist lens, is enormous, and any headway we are able to make in the future in terms of peace and international cooperation will involve moral principles that value and encourage ecumenical understanding and inter-religious dialogue.

Avoiding Dualistic Frameworks

If religion is central to culture, there should be agreement among scholars on a definition of religion, but no consensus exists. In order to provide distinction between religion and non-religion, some scholars appeal to a distinction between two realms of reality, the sacred and the secular, arguing that human involvement with the sacred defines the essence of religion.

The notion that religion can be defined as human interaction with the sacred has a long legacy in the West. This view, based upon a sacred-secular dualism, divides the world into two domains, the one containing all that is sacred and the other all that is profane. This understanding of religion was advanced and popularized in the middle of the twentieth century in Mircea Eliade's classic work *The Sacred and the Profane: The Nature of Religion*.

This distinction, based on an antiquated dualistic perspective long entrenched in the Western mindset, provides insuperable problems for many modern individuals, whose experience leads them to conceptualize the sacred (and therefore the supernatural, the spiritual, the metaphysical, and the nonmaterial) as a projection and/or an extension of society, thereby collapsing the sacred into the profane (the natural, physical, and material). This approach, while appearing reductionist, need not be dismissive of the sacred as a purely human construct. The intention can be cautionary about the inherent problems with the sacred-profane dualism and instructive in noting that this dualistic worldview is not a universal idea but a particularly Western (and monotheistic) construction.[1]

Religion as Noun or as Adjective

John Esposito, longtime professor and author of texts on world religions, highlights the difficulty of defining the term "religion" by asking his readers to engage in a thought experiment.[2] Suppose you could enter a time machine, he suggests, and be transported back to the city of Rome in the first century. He selects ancient Rome because the word "religion" has its roots in the Latin language of the Roman empire, and also because understanding how the Romans used the word might help us define what we mean by the term religion today.

Imagine that you are walking down a street in ancient Rome, and you approach a group of people standing on a corner. You ask: "What religion are you?" but they seem puzzled by the question. They understand the individual words, but the phrasing seems awkward and they do not understand what you are asking. So you rephrase the question:

---

1. Here I have in mind the attitude that dismisses, condemns, reduces, and stereotypes all nonmonotheistic beliefs and practices as "idolatrous," as though reducing all divinity and spirituality to one's own cherished singularity were not itself idolatrous.

2. Esposito, *World Religions Today*, 5–7.

"Are you religious?" This causes them to smile and reply, "Of course, isn't everyone?"

Why did they understand the second question but not the first?

According to Esposito, the first question treats the word religion as a noun describing distinct social bodies, such that each person understands himself or herself as identifying with and belonging to only one of those organization; if you are a Christian, you are by definition not a Jew or a Buddhist. But this way of understanding would be foreign to a person living in antiquity, and today it is foreign to many people living in Africa and Asia. Esposito points out that in Japan even today it is possible to be Buddhist, Taoist, Confucian, and Shinto all at the same time.

Once you rephrase the question from "What religion are you?" to "Are you religious?" you shift the function of the term religion from being a noun describing a distinct social group to being an adjective describing "an attitude toward the human condition—a way of seeing, acting, and experiencing all things."[3] According to Esposito, throughout history most people did not think of religion as a noun, as a separate reality they had to choose over and against another reality.

Esposito suggests that ancient Greeks and Romans viewed religion as a way of respecting all powers, natural and supernatural, that govern one's destiny, whether they be associated with war, fertility, or other aspects of society. Of course one would want all those forces on one's side. Anything else would be disastrous. For ancient Romans, as for nearly all other people throughout history, religion was essentially about divine favor and its influence on human destiny. According to this perspective, religion is not just about "spiritual" things, or deities, or God. Rather, religious attitudes are as diverse as the forms of power that people believe govern their destiny, whether these forms of power are related to nature, wealth, political power, individual wellbeing, or the forces of history.

Esposito's emphases seem spot-on. He is certainly correct to point out that the contemporary tendency to think of religion as a noun is rather unique to the contemporary Western world and that such a view represents a departure from what has been commonly understood by most people throughout history. Also, Esposito's attempt to reframe religion as an attitude toward power, in which he includes social, political, and economic power, suggests that religion must be understood as a

---

3. Esposito, *World Religions Today*, 6.

phenomenon pervading all of society, rather than as a distinct element existing in but separate from other elements of society.

The Etymology of the Word "Religion"

While it is true that many societies do not draw a clear line between culture and what scholars would call "religion," this does not mean that religion doesn't exist. What it does mean is that even when we think we have a handle on what religion is, we might be off base. Perhaps the most helpful starting point in understanding religion and its role in society is to examine the etymology of the word.

The classic explanation of the word religion, traced to the first-century BCE Roman orator Cicero, derives religion from the Latin word *relegere* (*re* + *lege*), which means "to read over again," in the sense of "consider carefully." Thus *religio*, the nominative of the Latin *religionem*, came to mean such things as "respect for what is sacred, reverence for the gods, sense of right, and religious observance." Religious law maintained the proprieties of divine honors, sacrifice to the gods, and proper ritual. Incorrect ritual and improper sacrifice were *vitia* (translated as "vice" in English), and the improper use or search of divine knowledge was *superstitio*. Neglecting the *religiones* (plural of *religio*) owed to the traditional gods was considered atheism, a charge leveled by ancient Romans at Christians as well as at Jews and Epicureans. The reason was clear: any moral deviation from acceptable religious norms was not only perverse, but it could bring harm to the state.

Another possible origin of "religion" is the Latin word *religare*, which means "to tie or to bind fast." Many modern writers favor this etymology, on the assumption that it helps to explain the power inherent in religion. Modern scholar Joseph Campbell favors a derivation from *ligo* (bind, connect), probably from a prefixed *re* (again) + *ligare*, meaning "to reconnect," a correlation made prominent by Augustine, based on an interpretation by Lactantius. The question immediately arises, to what should one reconnect? The answer is not clear. To theists, *religare* means to reconnect to God and to God's will for our lives. To polytheists *religare* implies reconnecting to the higher powers around us, and to the values espoused by social and religious leaders. To nature-based cultures, *religare* means to revere nature's ways, and to find one's place in the natural order. In each case, finding harmony with that which is considered to be ultimate in power and reverence, whether natural or supernatural, and with other human beings, is essential and mandatory. For monotheists, *religare* is best expressed in the double-love command, also known as the Great Commandment: "You shall love the Lord your God with all your heart, and with all your soul, and with all your mind, and with all your strength . . . and your neighbor as yourself" (Mark 12:30–31; cf. Deut 6:4; Lev 19:18).

A third possible origin of the term "religion" is the Latin word *religiens*, meaning "careful," in contrast to *negligens*, its opposite. In this sense, religion is a way of life lived thoughtfully and mindfully, not neglecting duties or devotion.

Healthy and "Junk" Religion

At their inception, world religions were healthy, wholesome, and beneficial. Over time, particularly as religions became institutionalized, that changed, so much so that we need to distinguish between "healthy" religion and "junk" religion. Healthy religion provides a foundational sense of awe. It re-enchants an otherwise empty universe. It encourages reverence toward all things, enabling people of faith to see the reflection of the divine image in the human, the animal, and the entire natural world, which now become enchanted, that is, inherently supernatural. When humans are fully alert in spirit, mind, and body, their identity transcends their imagination, and they can accomplish more than they suppose. Moments of awareness occur as a dawning of meaning, when the familiar suddenly becomes infused with new insight and possibilities, and when unfamiliar ideas challenge and pervade our consciousness. Such occasions feel like personal discoveries.

Instead of providing awe, reconnection, and awakening, junk religion—on both the left and the right of the religious spectrum—leads to sectarianism, ideological divisiveness, emotionalism, and even social and political hysteria. Similar to junk food because it only satisfies enough to gratify momentary desires, junk religion does not truly feed the intellect or the heart. Junk religion is usually characterized by dependence on the past, often leading to fear of the present as well as of the future. However, when religion leads us to encounter the divine, we are empowered to embrace not only the present but also the future without anxiety or fear. There is no fear of the present because it is viewed as full of potential. There is no fear of the future because a loving God is in charge. In addition, there is no fear of the past because the past has been healed and forgiven.

In authentic religion, people do not use theology to avoid reality or to fabricate a private, self-serving reality. Authentic believers let God lead them into the fullness of Reality—not into delusions, distrust, or conspiracy thinking, and not away from dilemmas, paradoxes, and uncertainties, but directly into the throes of their humanity.

Whatever reconstruction we need to undergo individually and as a society cannot be based on fear or on reaction. It must be based on a positive and fully human experience of God as a loving Presence. Healthy religion is ready to let God be God, and to embrace a future we do not yet understand—and no longer need to understand.

The Centrality and Meaning of Faith

If someone asked you to identify the essence of Christianity, where would you start? Conventional Christians, focusing on dogma, begin with belief in Jesus, the atonement, and the authority of scripture and the church. This approach, however, is antithetical to spirituality. Prior to the modern period, faith was not understood in this way. Faith was not about beliefs in one's head but about loyalty, allegiance, and trust in one's heart. Faith, of course, has always been central to Christianity, but an emphasis on faith as believing difficult things to be true is a relatively recent phenomenon in Christianity, the product of the last few hundred years.

Because religion by nature is primarily experiential, constructing religion on the foundation of belief leads to endless conflict, frustration, and unanswered questions. Children, of course, willingly accept belief, but as they go through adolescence and enter adulthood, many struggle with doubt and disbelief.

Faith, however, makes a better foundation and prepares one more adequately for life. Some readers may wonder about my distinction, because all through life they have equated faith with belief. But faith should not be equated with beliefs. Faith may reach conclusions about beliefs, but its foundation is experiential and relational rather than doctrinal. Based on experience, faith makes conscious choices that square with that experience.

In the history of Christianity, faith has four primary meanings.[4] The first of these sees faith primarily as a "matter of the head," whereas the remaining three understand faith as a "matter of the heart." Each meaning is described with a Latin term to show its antiquity, as well as how it is understood in English. For each term the opposite is given, for antonyms are often as illuminating as synonyms.

1. Faith as Assent (*assensus*). In this first sense faith means simply "belief," which we take to mean holding a certain set of "beliefs," that is, "believing" certain doctrines or dogmas to be true. This understanding of faith as belief is dominant today, both within the church and outside it. Its dominance in modern Western Christianity is due to the Protestant Reformation, which not only emphasized faith, but also produced numerous denominations, each defining itself by what it "believed," that is, by its distinctive doctrines or confessions.

This development also changed the meaning of the word "orthodoxy." Prior to the Protestant Reformation, orthodoxy referred to "right worship," meaning that those who practiced the liturgy correctly were orthodox. Following the Reformation, orthodoxy began to mean "right belief," and faith began to mean "believing the right things."

The birth of modern science and scientific ways of knowing in the Enlightenment also affected the meaning of "faith" and "believe." When Enlightenment thinkers began identifying truth with factuality, that is, as something verifiable, they began calling into question the reliability of the Bible and of many traditional Christian teachings. As a result, "faith" and "belief" came to be contrasted with knowledge and certainty. For skeptics, faith came to mean "opinion or conviction," something one turned to when knowledge ran out. For believers, faith is what one turned to when beliefs and knowledge conflict.

According to this understanding of faith, the opposite of faith as *assensus* is doubt or disbelief. In its fundamentalist permutation, those who doubt are said to lack faith, whereas those who disbelieve are said to have no faith. While this view is widespread, it puts the emphasis in the wrong place, for it suggests that what God really cares about is the beliefs in our heads, as if having "correct beliefs" is what will save us. In this respect, perhaps a better antonym of faith is "certainty."

Faith starts with the willingness to recognize and question the core mysteries at the heart of existence: why we exist at all and how to

---

4. This typology is adapted from Borg, *Heart of Christianity*, 28–37.

make meaning out of our existence. As a result, it puts on our radar the yearning for the answers to these ultimate questions and the consequent intuition that draws us to the words, ideas, and rituals of the religious tradition that attempts to answer them. We cannot know the answers to the ultimate questions as we can know scientific answers, which build bodies of knowledge over time. Religious answers are more like wisdom. Often they are paradoxical. Sometimes they require us to examine things backward: to increase by diminishing, to multiply by dividing, to hold on by letting go. With the habit of faith, we are willing to ponder such questions in our hearts and minds. Quoting Augustine, Aquinas says that belief is "giving assent to something one is still thinking about."

We turn now to the meanings of faith that are relational, those having more to do with the heart.

2. Faith as Trust (*fiducia*). In its second and higher sense, faith means "trust" in something or someone. In the Bible, it means radical trust in God. Significantly, it does not mean trusting in the truth of a set of statements about God, for that would simply be *assensus* under a different name. While our behavior is important, God seems to be less concerned with our actions than with our character, for our actions flow from our will: "For the Lord does not see as mortals see; they look on the outward appearance, but the Lord looks on the heart" (1 Sam 16:7).

Faith is like floating in a deep ocean. If you struggle, if you tense up and thrash about, you will eventually sink. But if you relax and trust, you will float. Like the story of Peter walking on the water with Jesus, when he began to be afraid, he began to sink. According to this meaning, the opposite of *fiducia* is not doubt or disbelief, but mistrust, which results in worry and anxiety. Four times in the extended passage from Matthew's Sermon on the Mount, Jesus says to his hearers, "Do not worry," and then adds, "You of little faith" (Matt 6:25–34). Lack of trust and anxiety go together; if you are anxious, you have little faith.

3. Faith as Faithfulness (*fidelitas*). In the Bible, faith is the trustful acceptance of God's promises, particularly of God's desire to bless all peoples and nations of the world. But faith is also trust in God's faithfulness to the promise, that is, in God's ability to deliver Good News to everyone, something that God accomplishes through Jesus Christ and his followers. Because God is steadfast and faithful, we too are called to faithfulness. *Fidelitas* does not mean faithfulness to beliefs about God, whether biblical, creedal, or doctrinal. Rather it refers to radical centering in the God to whom the Bible and creeds and doctrines point.

The English equivalent to *fidelitas* is "fidelity." Faith as fidelity means loyalty, allegiance, the commitment of the self at its deepest level. Its opposite is not doubt or disbelief. Rather, as in human relationships, its opposite is infidelity, being unfaithful to our relationship with God. To use a striking biblical metaphor, the opposite of this meaning of faith is adultery. Another vivid biblical term for infidelity to God is idolatry, meaning not so much the worship of idols as false gods, but centering in something finite rather than the sacred, which is infinite and beyond all images. As the opposite of idolatry, faith means being loyal to God "and not to the seductive would-be lords of our lives," whether one's nation, affluence, achievement, family, or desire.[5]

In the Hebrew Bible, faith as fidelity is the meaning of the first of the Ten Commandments: "You shall have no other gods before me." In the New Testament, it is the meaning of the Great Commandment: "You shall love the Lord your God with all your heart, soul, mind, and strength." This commandment is followed immediately by the exhortation to "love your neighbor as yourself." *Fidelitas* means being faithful to these two great relationships: God and your neighbor. And one's neighbor, as Jesus explains in the parable of the Good Samaritan, is first and foremost the person who is in need of help (Luke 10:29–37).

One is faithful to God, therefore, by being attentive to these two primary relationships. We are attentive to God through worship, prayer, and practice, and faithful to our neighbor through a life of compassion and justice. To be faithful to God also means to love that which God loves, which includes the whole of creation.

4. Faith as Vision (*visio*). As the English word "vision" suggests, faith is a way of seeing reality, and how we view the whole affects how we respond to life. There are basically three ways we can see the whole:

- We can see reality as *hostile and threatening*, and therefore respond to life defensively, doing whatever we can to survive, for that is all that matters. Many forms of popular religion have viewed reality this way: God (or Life, or Nature) is going to get us, unless we behave the right way, practice the correct rituals, offer the right sacrifices, or believe the right things;.

- We can see reality as *indifferent* to human purposes and ends. Although this response to life will be less anxious than that of the first way, we are still likely to be defensive and precautionary. We

---

5. Borg, *Heart of Christianity*, 33.

respond by building up whatever security we can, even enjoying and seeking to take care of the world, but ultimately we are likely to be concerned primarily for ourselves and those who are most important to us.

- We can see reality as *life-giving, nourishing, and full of promise*. To use a traditional theological term, to see reality as filled with wonder and beauty, and to nourish and spread this goodness, leads to radical trust. It frees us from the anxiety, self-preoccupation, and concern to protect the self with systems of security that mark the first two viewpoints. It leads to the ability to love and to be present to the moment. It generates a commitment to spend oneself for the sake of a vision that extends beyond ourselves. To use Paul's words, it leads to a life marked by the "fruit of the Spirit": love, joy, peace, patience, kindness, generosity, faithfulness, gentleness, and self-control" (Gal 5:22–23). These qualities are the result of a way of life that Paul characterizes as "freedom" (Gal 5:1); freedom *from* evil and from allegiance to false authorities; freedom *for* love. For Paul, faith becomes active "through love" (Gal 5:6).

To understanding faith as *visio* is to see reality as gracious; its opposite, un-faith, views reality as hostile and indifferent. This meaning of faith is closely related to *fiducia*, to faith as trust. Trust and vision go together; trust in God—the God of promise and faithfulness—and how we view God go together. In this way of life, radical centering in God leads to a deepening trust that transforms the way we view reality and live our lives. Seeing, living, trusting, and centering are all related in complex and salutary ways.

As we have noted, faith is relational, but this does not mean that beliefs don't matter. There are affirmations that are central to the Christian faith, affirmations such as the reality of God, the centrality of Jesus, and the significance of the Bible. These beliefs are essential, not only for Christians, but for people of all faiths, when properly understood. Faith as a way of seeing at the deepest level requires avoiding the human tendency toward excessive precision and certitude. Christian theology has often been plagued by both—the desire to know too much and to know it too precisely. Our minds tell us that such knowledge is not possible—perhaps not even desirable—and people cannot easily give their heart to something that their mind rejects. Properly understood, a deep but humble understanding of Christian faith as *assensus* is close to faith as *visio*. As we have seen, biblical and theological faith need not be viewed as assent to narrow propositions or as fulfilling specific requirements, but as a persuasive and compelling way of seeing reality.

While faith involves the mind, faith is primarily the way of the heart. Given the premodern meaning of "believe," to believe in God is to love God and to love that which God loves. The Christian life is as simple and challenging as that.

Faith and the Human Brain

As Brian McLaren explains in *Faith After Doubt*, the human brain functions like a three-member committee.[6] Understanding the brain in this manner is not to simplify the brain's complexity, for each primary module of this brain committee includes many distinct submodules that in turn contain even smaller submodules.

The brain's oldest primary module, sometimes called the reptilian brain, includes the brain stem and cerebellum. This *instinctive brain*, present before birth, controls the basic bodily functions. Its job is to keep us alive in a dangerous world. Shortly after birth, a second member of the brain committee becomes engaged. This *intuitive brain*, sometimes called the mammalian or limbic brain, orients us toward attachment by generating emotions that strengthen relationships necessary for our survival.

The limbic system, which may be thought of as the primary emotional controller of the brain, is comprised of several different structures. It includes the amygdala, which functions as a watchdog in the brain. The amygdala turns on when anything of emotional importance—positive or negative—occurs in our environment. Another structure of the limbic system is the hippocampus, which functions as a diplomat of the brain. It helps to regulate our emotional responses so that we don't become too extreme in one way or another. Another important structure in the limbic system is the hypothalamus, which regulates our hormones, crucial in determining how our body reacts to the external world and to the brain.

From an early age, the instinctive and intuitive modules are already working together, keeping us safe and keeping us connected with those upon whom our survival depends. Around the age of two, the third brain committee member, consisting of the neocortex and its components, begins to assert itself. This *intellectual brain*, often called the primate brain,

---

6. McLaren, *Faith After Doubt*, 15–23.

is the logical, rational, analytical member of one's brain committee. This module is the seat of intellect, and it enables us to use language and to think critically and creatively.

People also refer to these three committee member as the gut (the instinctive brain), the heart (the intuitive brain), and the head (the intellectual brain). They are also known as the survival module, the relational module, and the meaning module. Thus, "when we speak of healthy, mature, or well-rounded human beings, we are referring to people who integrate their survival, belonging, and meaning modules (and all their submodules) in ways that bring benefit and pleasure to themselves and others."[7]

The brain is divided into four basic lobes: the occipital love in the back of the brain, the frontal lobe in the front part of the brain, the temporal lobe along the side of the brain, and the parietal lobe toward the back top part of the brain. These different association areas take information from different neurons to construct our relation to the external world. The parietal lobe (the orientation area of the brain) is relevant to religious or spiritual experiences. For example, patterns at work in the orientation area influence the way we think about ourselves. Other cognitive functions of the brain help us with quantitative thinking, whereby numbers are given meaning and importance, or with binary thinking, whereby we determine opposites and polarities such as what is right and wrong. Likewise, the causal functioning part of the brain is activated when we consider cause and effect in the world, including ideas about God as Creator; the existential function in the brain tells us whether something is real or not; the reductionistic function breaks thing into component parts; and the holistic function binds things together. When people have mystical experiences, such as a sense of oneness or unity in the cosmos, the holistic function is involved. Lastly, the abstract function in the brain allows us to think about things abstractly, a quality crucial for the philosophical, religious, and theological ideas that we hold.[8]

When we think about faith, it is important to do so holistically, as it involves the whole brain. When we think of faith as Assent, for instance, we are limiting the concept to our meaning/intellect module. To engage with the stories of faith, as well as the doctrines or statements of faith based upon the songs, poetry, stories, symbols, and history of a religious

---

7. McLaren, *Faith After Doubt*, 17.
8. Newberg, *Spiritual Brain*, 18–22.

tradition, is to engage the more rational, analytical, and independent member of the brain committee. However, that is not the whole story. We learn and practice faith in families and communities of faith, and that engages the intuitive/belonging module as well. As McLaren notes, without our existential need for belonging, religion and faith systems may never have developed. Finally, many of us see faith as a matter of survival, in this life and beyond, which energizes the survival module as well. In this respect, faith is a matter of head, heart, and gut; of meaning, belonging, and survival; of intellect, intuition, and instinct. Faith is a whole-brain and whole-self endeavor.

This is not to say, however, that faith engages people in the same ways. For example, some people don't think much about their faith. For them, it is primarily a matter of belonging or of survival. They don't question their faith intellectually or find much room for doubt, because for them, the conceptual side of faith simply isn't that important. For such people, faith is as essential as eating and breathing; to question or change it is unthinkable. Others, of course, are hard-wired to question, analyze, think, and even to doubt with regularity. Life-long learning is what makes them tick; thinking and pondering are essential to their existence. However one functions and thrives, it is important to remember that the three processes of the brain—meaning, belonging, and surviving—are all interrelated. Our meaning module's independent thought processes are constantly being monitored and even censored by our belonging and survival modules. And when the meaning and belonging modules are out of alignment, with one feeling safe and the other feeling insecure, or both feeling insecure or unstable, we can be sure that the third and senior member of our brain committee, the survival module, is reflexively emitting stress hormones like adrenaline, cortisol, and norepinephrine. These hormones prepare us to fight, flee, freeze, or appease external and even internal dangers or threats, real or perceived. Our survival module seems to have a kind of veto power in matters of belief, making it nearly impossible to change behavioral or thought patterns. Thus, when transformational behavior occurs or beliefs change, such as found in second half of life thinking and living, they can be attributed to divine or supernatural grace.

Questions for Discussion and Reflection

1. Define "dualistic thinking," and in a few sentences assess its attractiveness to religious individuals as well as its disadvantage as a way of viewing reality.
2. In your estimation, how helpful is Esposito's distinction between speaking of religion as noun or as adjective? Which approach do you favor? Why?
3. Based on the etymology of the term "religion," which of the three derivations do you find most helpful? Support your answer.
4. In light of the textual discussion of the three etymological derivations of the term "religion," take a few moments to answer the following questions:
    a. What do I hold sacred in my life? How do I show respect for the sacred in my life?
    b. What do I consider to be "ultimate" in the universe in terms of power and reverence? How can I find harmony with this power?
    c. Am I living thoughtfully and mindfully? How do I fall short of that mark? How can I live more intentionally? Am I lacking in discipline or devotion?
5. In your own words, explain the role of faith in spiritual transformation.
6. If faith is said to be related to the intellect, what is the first step in the renewal of one's mind?
7. Explain how the meaning of the word "belief" has changed since biblical times.
8. Assess the usefulness of McLaren's notion that faith is a byproduct of the brain's three-member committee. In your estimation, what is the influence of one's brain on one's spirituality? Explain your answer.

Chapter 5

Rethinking Belief in God[1]

GIVEN THE QUANDARY WE face, socially and environmentally, exacerbated by our complicity with racism and our propensity for exploiting natural resources, America needs help. Ironically, if solutions exist, they must come not from exclusively American expertise—from uniquely modern, scientific, or Christian values—but from the Perennial Tradition, from peoples, beliefs, and customs North Americans have traditionally overlooked, discarded, or displaced in their strident surge onward.

When I speak of the Perennial Tradition, sometimes called Perennial Philosophy or simply "the wisdom tradition," I am referring to the view that the world's major religions share common teachings, and that these truths transcend culture, time, and place. Jews, Christians, or members of any specific religion, should not feel they were the first to know God's eternal patterns and presence. After all, those patterns are perfectly plain, because God has made it plain. "Ever since the creation of the world [God's] eternal power and divine nature, invisible though they are, have been understood and seen through the things [God] has made" (Rom 1:19–20). How else could it be? How could any God worthy of the name squeeze Being itself into any specific timeframe, culture, or vocabulary? That is what we mean by the Perennial Tradition.

People who value perennial wisdom share core existential questions with other human beings, only they do not confine their search for answers to any one religion. What I call "core existential questions,"

---

1. The material in this chapter is adapted from chapters 3–4 of my book, *Walking on Water*. While this topic occupies a necessary place in our discussion, it is intended primarily for those not otherwise familiar with my writings.

what philosophers call "ultimate questions," can be reduced to four: (1) "Is there an ultimate reality?" (2) "Can I relate to that reality?" (3) "How does that relationship affect the way I live?" and (4) "What can I hope for?" Because these questions never go away, they form the heart of almost every spiritual quest.

It is the main business of religion to answer life's existential questions. And this is why, even when we try to distance ourselves from it, we remain intrigued by religion. Religion responds to the preoccupations that arise when life comes up against barriers beyond which ordinary—including scientific—ways of coping cannot take us. For our purposes, therefore, religions may be understood very simply as pathways or "route-findings" through the ultimate limits on our lives. These limits include not only death and meaninglessness but also anything that threatens our wellbeing, anything that stands between us and lasting peace or happiness.

To accomplish this task, every generation of believers benefits by re-examining its theology, thereby providing society with vision. A useful place to start is the Perennial Tradition, by which I mean not the distinct perspectives of other religious traditions—for the goal of spiritual transformation is a deeper understanding of one's own faith tradition, not conversion to some alternative religious tradition—but rather the congruence of values and beliefs (absolutes) across cultures, those unchanging beliefs that unite human traditions that seek wisdom in ancient texts and modes of life. According to perennial wisdom, every religious tradition, when one explores its mystical side, articulates common answers to humanity's existential questions, answers that emerge repeatedly throughout human history and across human culture.

Agostino Steuco (1497–1548), likely the first to coin the phrase "perennial philosophy," used it with reference to four timeless truths taught by the great sages and mystics of every civilization throughout human history:

1. There is only one ultimate Reality—called by many names, including God, Tao, Allah, Brahman, Emptiness, or Great Spirit—that is the source and substance of all existence.

2. Each human being is a manifestation of this Reality, though most identify with a smaller, culturally conditioned individual ego.

3. This identification with the individualized self gives rise to needless suffering and anxiety, leading to cross-cultural competition and violence.

4. Identifying with one's True Self, that is, realizing that one's true nature is a manifestation of the singular Reality, gives rise to peace and love, enabling human beings to engage others with compassion and justice.[2]

The famous writer James Michener captured the meaning of the religious quest when he concluded *The Source*, his masterful saga of the Holy Land, with the haunting words attributed to his character Ilan Eliav, an Israeli archaeologist, "We seek God so earnestly . . . not to find Him but to discover ourselves."[3]

Ultimate Reality: The Source and Substance of all Existence

Perennial wisdom, found in most human cultures, religions, and civilizations, begins not with time, space, matter, or even with ontology (speculation about divine essence or Being), but with a common singularity we call Unity, or better yet, Mystery. As Lao Tzu, the sixth-century BCE author of the *Tao Te Ching*, says in his opening poem, "The Tao that can be named is not the eternal Tao. The name that can be named is not the eternal name . . . Darkness within darkness. The gate to all mystery."

The Perennial Tradition says that there is a capacity for divine reality inside all humans, but we initially cannot see what we are looking for because what we are looking for is doing the looking. God, the name most of us give to Ultimate Reality, is never an object to be found or possessed as we find other objects, but the One who shares our deepest subjectivity by virtue of being only Subject, never object. Furthermore, we do not see things as *they* are, but rather we see things as *we* are, through our own level of development and consciousness. This affects not only how we view Reality, but also how we read scripture. We see the text through our available eyes. Punitive people love punitive texts; loving people hear in the same text calls to discernment, clarity, choice, and decision. In the world of spirituality, nondualists are the only experts.

2. Shapiro, *Perennial Wisdom*, xiv.
3. Michener, *Source*, 909.

More than with any other personality trait in our lives, all-or-nothing thinking causes huge mistakes and bad judgments. It results in withholding love, misinterpreting situations, and hurting both others and ourselves. This pattern of dualistic or polarity thinking is deeply entrenched in most of us, despite its severe limitations. Dualistic thinking is not wrong or bad in itself—in fact, it is necessary in most situations. However, it is completely inadequate for the major questions and dilemmas of life.

Dualistic people use knowledge, even religious knowledge, for the purposes of ego enhancement, shaming, and the control of others and themselves, for it works very well in that way. Nondual people use knowledge for the transformation of persons and structures, but especially to experience transformation, seeing reality with a new eye and heart.

This realization helps to explain the great paradox we all must face—and embrace—that God is both perfectly hidden and perfectly revealed in all things. God has written the pattern in things as they are, and yet we never see the full pattern without divine assistance. Thus, faith (trust in the divine) is always necessary to see what is "natural."

Despite their commonality, the many names for the Ultimate Reality, viewed culturally, theologically, and religiously, do not mean the same thing. For example, in the context of Islam, Allah has no son, chooses Muhammad as his final prophet, and the Qur'an as final revelation. In the context of Christianity, God has a son, knows nothing about Muhammad, and does not reveal the Qur'an. Similarly, the Jewish God knows nothing of Jesus and has nothing to do with the New Testament, which Christians regard as the Word of God. Likewise, Krishna, God for many Hindus, has nothing to do with the Hebrew Bible, the Greek New Testament, or the Arabic Qur'an. If you wish to understand Krishna, you must read the Bhagavad Gita, the revelation of Lord Krishna to Arjuna, about which the Jewish, Christian, and Muslim Gods know nothing.

Hence, in the context of comparative religion, it is wrong to claim that all Gods are the same, or that all Gods are variations of a specific context. If you want to study Allah, study Islam. If you want to learn about Krishna, Vishnu, Shiva, and the rest of the Gods of India, study the many schools of Hinduism. In the study of world religions, each deity must be allowed to speak in its own way, or at least to reflect the values of its priests, prophets, sages, and gurus.

The Perennial Tradition, however, does not seek such distinctions. Rather, it sifts through the scriptures and teachings of many cultures looking for those teachings that transcend the limits of specific cultures and point to the Reality that cannot be named, defined, or figured out. Augustine, the great fifth-century theologian, articulated that very idea when he declared, "*Si comprehenderis, non est Deus*" (If you understand, then what you understand is not God). God, it seems, cannot really be known, but only related to.

Such teaching, central to scripture, is regularly overlooked by people committed to religious uniqueness or denominational distinctives. Due to scripture's narrative nature, essential teachings about God are not dealt with abstractly, dogmatically, or systematically, but rather in pastoral or social settings, such as by caring for the poor and needy (Jer 22:16) and by loving fellow human beings in general (1 John 4:20; see also Jas 1:27).

Alternatively, as mystics assert, we know God by loving God, by trusting God, by placing our hope in God. Such relating is always non-possessive, a non-objectified way of knowing. It is always I-Thou and never I-It, to use Martin Buber's insightful perspective. As Marion Zimmer Bradley notes in her novels, God appears to us as we can best understand. Nevertheless, all the gods are one God, and all the goddesses are one Goddess, and together they are one; yet to each their own path, and the truth within.[4]

Is the Perennial Tradition, the perspective that all the world's religions share a single truth or origin, consonant with Christianity? For many, this perspective is false, misleading, and heretical. For others, however, it is not only compatible with Christianity, but it represents an essential and oft overlooked aspect of Christianity, perhaps its deepest insight and teaching.

A person's view of God is vital because it serves as a lens through which people view reality, influencing their perspective of life, the cosmos, others, and of themselves. As one's view of self provides a microcosm of reality, so one's view of God serves as a macrocosm of that reality. If one's view of God is positive—such as lover or friend—then the universe seems benevolent, others are valued, and the self is considered good. However, if one's view of God is negative—such as angry antagonist or vindictive judge—then the universe seems harsh, others are devalued, and the self is considered evil or sinful.

Theology is "talk about God." The majority of people who use the term "God," particularly in the Western world, have in mind a theistic

---

4. Bradley, *Mists of Avalon*, x–xi.

concept of God, meaning an all-powerful and supreme ruler of the universe. Supernatural theism, by implication, includes the view that all finite things are dependent in some way on this ultimate reality, a reality generally described in personal terms. After all, imaging God as a personal being is very common in the Bible. It is also the natural language of worship and prayer, and there is nothing wrong with it in such contexts. A transcendent reality that does not possess at the very least those qualities that constitute the dignity of human beings, qualities such as intelligence, feeling, freedom, power, initiative, and creativity, could not adequately inspire trust or reverence in human beings. In this sense, God would have to be "personal" to be God. It is doubtful whether believers could worship something that does not have at least the stature of personality.

While the idea of a "personal God" is beneficial in that it makes God relational and accessible to humanity, the extremes of this position, such as presented in the Hebrew scriptures, raise insuperable problems for people in the modern era. This God fights wars and defeats enemies, chooses people and works through them, sends storms, heals the sick, spares the dying, rewards goodness, and punishes evil. Many people have trouble intellectually with these anthropomorphic renderings of God and with the seeming irrationality of belief in a personal God. While only the most traditional believers and the most literal readers of scripture believe such things anymore, this deity remains the primary object and substance of the Christian church's faith. It is this understanding of God that is becoming meaningless to increasing numbers in the modern world.

While it is attractive to speak of intimacy with God and accessibility to God, religious philosophers have long warned against ascribing human qualities and attributing human feelings to God. Still, the joy of familiarity with God and the need to recognize and be recognized by God override the philosopher's critique. There is, however, a critical flaw in this perspective: Once we conceive of God as a person like ourselves, God becomes open to criticism.

To protect God, apologists and theologians urge us to discard this way of thinking. God is not like us, says twentieth-century theologian Karl Barth; God is "Totally Other." This understanding views God as different not only in degree but also in kind. Humans can only speak of God indirectly, says thirteenth-century theologian Thomas Aquinas, for they cannot "know" God directly. Humans can only speak of God or "know" God indirectly, by saying what God is not (the *via negativa*), or by saying what God is like, thereby resorting to analogies or metaphors (the *via analogia*).

Rethinking Belief in God

In using models of transcendence, whereby God is said to be all-knowing, all-powerful, and all-good, we instinctively know that we are not referring to the same kind of qualities we understand when speaking of attributes in humans. Does this mean, then, that God cannot be said to be moral in the manner that we are said to be moral? If so, that raises deep resentments. We hear it in the outburst of the philosopher John Stuart Mill: "I will call no being good who is not what I mean when I apply the epithet to my fellow creatures, and if such a being can sentence me to hell, to hell I will go."[5]

In his publication, *The Sins of Scripture*, Bishop John Shelby Spong examines biblical moral principles attributed to the will of God and concludes that those who wish to base their morality literally on the Bible have either not read it or not understood it. Bishop Spong spoke forcefully and shockingly when he wrote:

> There is no supernatural God who lives above the sky or beyond the universe. There is no supernatural God who can be understood as animating spirit, Earth Mother, masculine tribal deity or external monotheistic being. There is no parental deity watching over us from whom we can expect help. There is no deity whom we can flatter into acting favorably or manipulate by being good. There are no record books and no heavenly judge keeping them to serve as the basis on which human beings will be rewarded or punished. There is also no way that life can be made to be fair or that a divine figure can be blamed for its unfairness. Heaven and hell are human constructs designed to make fair in some ultimate way the unfairness of life. The idea that in an afterlife the unfairness of this world will be rectified is a pious dream, a toe dip into unreality. Life is lived at the whim of luck and chance, and no one can earn the good fortune of luck and chance.[6]

With Spong, I too recoil at these words, for the traditional understanding of God has been my guide from the beginning. Unlike some who have concluded that God is no more, Spong does not mean to say that God once existed but has since died. Nor does he mean to say that there is no God. What he calls "God" is real, only not as popularly conceived.[7]

---

5. Cited by Schulweis, *Those Who Can't Believe*, 132.

6. Spong, *Eternal Life*, 121–22.

7. The conventional understanding of God, based in part on medieval debates and the language of certain classical theologians, attributes to deity such qualities as impassibility (that God cannot experience pain and suffering), transcendence (that

But what are the alternatives? Is atheism (a-theism) the only alternative to theism? Technically, of course, there are numerous options, including polytheism (the belief that there are numerous deities), pantheism (the belief that God is in everything for everything is divine), henotheism (the notion of worshipping a territorial god, conceived as one god among many), animism (the belief that nature is filled with spirits or souls, which must be worshipped or appeased), and panentheism.

Understanding God Panentheistically

Many people today are finding the case for panentheism increasingly attractive in an age of science and reason. One can find historical traces of panentheism in both Western and Eastern orthodox theology, though the word itself was popularized by English philosopher Alfred North Whitehead (1861–1947). Panentheism is not the same as pantheism, the concept that "all things are God." Rather, pan*en*theism is the concept that "all things are *in* God." Panentheism views God not as a supernatural being separate from the universe, beyond nature and history, but as the encompassing Spirit around us and within us. According to this conception, God is more than the universe, yet the universe is in God. Viewed spatially, God is not "out there" but "right here." Whereas supernatural theism emphasizes God's transcendence—God's otherness, God as more than the universe—panentheism affirms both the transcendence and immanence of God. It does not deny or subordinate one in order to affirm the other. For panentheism, God is both more than the universe and yet everywhere present in the universe.

In this regard, panentheism is located between traditional theism and pantheism. As David Ray Griffin describes it, panentheism "combines features of both pantheism, which regards God as 'essentially immanent and in no way transcendent,' and traditional theism, which regards God 'as essentially transcendent and only accidentally immanent.'"[8] Griffin's work helps to explain why panentheism isn't just pantheism with a new name: "Panentheism is crucially different from pantheism because God transcends the universe in the sense that God has God's own creative

---

God is eternal and unchanging and largely unrelated to this world), and omnipotence (unlimited in power and capable of doing all things). Overall, such views are unbiblical and, with regard to the concept of "omnipotence," philosophically indefensible.

8. Griffin, *Reenchantment*, 141.

power, distinct from that of the universe of finite actualities. Hence, each finite actual entity has its own creativity with which to exercise some degree of self-determination, so that it transcends the divine influence upon it."[9]

Theologians in various traditions have offered different ways of defining and modeling this God-world relationship. According to the influential German evangelical theologian Jürgen Moltmann, in the panentheistic view God, having created the world, also dwells in it, and conversely the world which he has created exists in him. He writes of God "making space," a *nothing* (*nihil*) to which God gives being (*creatio ex nihilo*). "God does not create merely by calling something into existence . . . In a more profound sense he 'creates' by letting-be, by making room, by withdrawing himself."[10] Moltmann's language expresses the idea of the world, including humanity, as "enveloped by God without losing its true distinctiveness."[11] Consonant with Moltmann's theology, Anglican theologian Arthur Peacocke writes that "God is best conceived of as the circumambient [i.e., surrounding] reality enclosing all existing entities, structures and processes, and as operating in and through all, while being 'more' than all. Hence, all that is not God has its existence within God's operation and Being."[12] Other panentheistic models have been suggested, but all reveal a common theme: the world is given existence, energy, life, nourishment, and continuous creation by the God in whom "we live and move and have our being" (Acts 17:28).

Fortunately there are alternatives to the concept of theism, for "theism" and "God" need not be the same. Supernatural theism is but one human definition of God. Panentheists affirm that "God" does not refer to a supernatural being "in heaven," apart from nature, but rather to the sacred at the center of existence, the holy mystery that is around us and within us. Panentheism affirms the centrality of mystery in the universe and the possibility of relating intellectually and experientially to that mystery. It is possible, then, to be an agnostic or even an atheist regarding the God of supernatural theism and yet be a believer in God in the way offered by panentheism.

---

9. Griffin, *Reenchantment*, 142.
10. Moltmann, *God in Creation*, 88–89.
11. Clayton and Peacocke, *In Whom We Live*, 145.
12. Clayton and Peacocke, *In Whom We Live*, 146.

Alfred North Whitehead characterized God's relationship to the world as that of a "Persuasive Lover;" and others have offered variations on Whitehead's theme. The love relationship is an apt metaphor, for love is the fundamental and most intimate of relationships. Two qualities make this analogy particularly attractive: (1) that the essence of love is persuasive rather than coercive, and (2) that the experience of the beloved is to flourish and grow and emerge into fullness of life as a result of being loved. If this is so in human experience, then in a much more profound way God's unconditional love for the creation must be such as to invite the creation into ever more complex levels of being. To accomplish this, the God of infinite love freely accepts the integrity of nature, its processes and its laws, thereby inviting the world through the complex interplay of all of its elements to emerge into more novel forms and greater beauty through the evolutionary process.

God as Spirit

While traditional theists have been one-sided in speaking of the remoteness of God from the ordinary realm of experience, mystics have emphasized the "nearness" of the sacred. In fact, because there is no contradiction between the absence and the nearness of God, God's absence may even be understood as essential for the sake of the nearness. By not intruding into or forcing itself upon the world and personal subjects, the divine mystery can be understood as caringly involved with the world. Concerned that the world not lose its integrity by being absorbed into the divine or diluted into an overbearing divine "presence," God may be seen to "withdraw" from the world and from persons in order to let them be. This withdrawal, this self-absenting of God, however, is not abdication but rather essential in order to give the world its autonomy and human subjects their freedom. In this sense the absence and inscrutability of mystery may be understood as the other side of its intimacy with us.[13]

In his accessible book titled *The God We Never Knew*, biblical scholar Marcus Borg examined the variety of images of God in the biblical and Christian traditions and discerned therein two primary "models":

1. The *"monarchical model,"* which clusters images of God as king, lord, and father. This approach leads to what Borg calls a "performance model" of the Christian life.

13. Haught, *What is God?*, 130–31.

2. The "*Spirit model*," which clusters images of God that point to intimate relationship and belonging. This model leads to a "relational model" of the Christian life.

Both models, Borg discovered, are found throughout all periods of Christian history, though the first is more common. From roughly the fourth century—when Christianity became the dominant religion of Western culture—through the present, the monarchical model has dominated. But alongside it, as an alternative voice, the Spirit model has also persisted. These models reflect two different voices within the Christian tradition.

The monarchical model portrays God as male, as all-powerful, as lawgiver, and as judge. Images of God in this model suggest that God is distant. Within this model, humans have offended divine majesty and deserve judgment. But because God loves his subjects, God creates a way for his people to escape the punishment they deserve: through appropriate sacrifice and true repentance. In the royal theology of ancient Israel, atonement was institutionalized in temple rituals. In the Christian version of the monarchical model, the king's (Lord's) love is seen especially in Jesus. Because God loves us, he sends his son into the world to die on a cross as the sacrifice that makes our forgiveness possible.[14]

The Spirit model, as used in the Bible, is broader than the specific Christian doctrine of "the Holy Spirit," which sees the Spirit as one aspect of God. In the Bible, Spirit is used comprehensively to refer to God's presence in creation, in the history of Israel, and in the life of Jesus and the early church. While the monarchical model also affirms that God is Spirit, of course, and that affirmation can be a source of confusion that limits our understanding of God, there is a difference. When Spirit is assimilated to the monarchical model, God is not Spirit but a spirit—that is, a spiritual being out there, not here. But when Spirit is set free from the monarchical understanding, Spirit retains the suggestive meanings associated with breath and wind: God is the encompassing Spirit both within and outside us.[15]

The images of God associated with the Spirit model dramatically affect how we think of the Christian life. Rather than God as a distant being with whom we might spend eternity, Spirit—the sacred—is right here. Rather than sin and guilt being the central dynamic of the Christian life, the central dynamic becomes relationship—with God, the world, and each other.

14. Borg, *God We Never Knew*, 63–64.
15. Borg, *God We Never Knew*, 72.

The mystics of every religious tradition, following the Spirit model rather than the monarchical model, have always spoken out against specific definitions of God. The Western mystics appear to have assumed that a personal God was only a stage, and an inferior one at that, in human religious development. The mystical portrait of God was first imaginative, and then ineffable. It involved an interior journey, not an exterior one. In the mystical tradition, no one can claim objectivity for his or her insight. Each person is called to journey into the mystery of God along the pathway of his or her own expanding personhood. Every person is thus capable of being a theophany, as sign of God's presence; but no one person, institution, or way of life can exhaust this revelation. God, for the mystics, is found at the depths of life, working in and through the being of this world, calling all nature to its deepest potential.

Alfred North Whitehead, who began his professional life as a mathematician, laid out the theological framework for perceiving God not as a divine being external to the universe, but as a divine process coming into being within the life of this world. This conception of God as existing with all of reality, not prior to it, became known as process theology. Dietrich Bonhoeffer called the world to something he named "religionless Christianity," suggesting in his letters, written from prison as he awaited his execution by the Third Reich, that Christians need to live in this world "as if there were no God." His death as a martyr prevented him from conceptualizing further the implications of his hypothesis, but a religionless—perhaps even a nontheistic or godless—Christianity appeared on the horizon of his thinking.

Paul Tillich, himself a refugee from Nazi Germany, proposed as far back as the 1930s and 1940s that Western Christians should abandon the external height images in which the theistic God had historically been perceived, replacing them with internal depth images of a deity not apart from us but the very core and ground of all that is. This God was not a person, but rather was the mystical presence in which all personhood could flourish. This God was not a being but rather the power that called being forth in all creatures. This God was not an external, personal force that could be invoked but rather an internal reality that, when confronted, opened us to the meaning of life itself.[16] Tillich, who believed that the word "God" had been distorted by the inadequate images of the past, was convinced that those images must die before the word "God" could ever

---

16. Spong, *Christianity Must Change*, 64.

be used again with meaning. He urged a moratorium on the use of the word "God" for at least a hundred years.

Following Tillich, Bishop Spong provides a model that integrates the Christian doctrine of the Trinity with this understanding of God. The meaning of God, according to his conception, is understood as (1) the source of life, (2) the source of love, and (3) the ground of being. He finds in this triune understanding a portrait of God embodied in Jesus of Nazareth, a whole human being who lived fully, loved lavishly, and had the courage to be himself under every circumstance.

So the call of this internal God found in our depths becomes primarily a call into being, a call that is not unique to religion. It is a call that refocuses what has been known as the religious dimension. In this scenario, the task of the church becomes less that of indoctrinating or relating people to an external divine power and more that of providing opportunities for people to touch the infinite center of all things and to fulfill all their potential. This understanding of God places a premium on the church's vocation to oppose anything that prevents us from the fullest expression of our humanity.

We are learning that "meaning" is not external to life but must be discovered in our own depths and imposed on life by an act of our own will. We are being made aware that life is not fair and will not necessarily be made fair either in this life or in any other. So we have to decide how we will live now with this reality. One thing is certain: the journey of faith must go forward.

Years ago, J. B. Phillips, translator of the celebrated *New Testament in Modern English* (1958), wrote a small volume titled *Your God is Too Small*. If, in describing our understanding of God, we are found to be heterodox, I trust it will be because our God is too big rather than too small. If our views differ from the mainstream of current Christian orthodoxy, we may find that they belong to that tradition of Christian orthodoxy described as apophatic,[17] rather than in the prevalent Western theological tradition characterized as kataphatic.[18]

---

17. The term "apophatic" refers to ways of knowing God that are direct and not mediated. Apophatics reflect an intuitive form of spirituality, which views God as ineffable and indescribable. Apophatics are comfortable with ambiguity and, when speaking of God, they prefer terms such as Mystery or Spirit. They prefer to worship God in silence or by striving for justice and peace in the world.

18. The term "kataphatic" refers to ways of knowing God that are indirect and mediated. Kataphatics reflect a sensate form of spirituality, which prefers concrete images of God. Kataphatics are often divided into two groups: those who prefer to worship

Questions for Discussion and Reflection

1. In your own words, define "Perennial Philosophy" or "wisdom tradition." Are these concepts identical or merely similar? Explain your answer.
2. In your own words, name the four existential or ultimate questions addressed by Perennial Philosophy. Why are these questions central to the spiritual quest? Are there other questions or issues you would add to the list? Explain your answer.
3. Explain the difference between viewing Ultimate Reality (God) as Subject or as object.
4. Assess the validity of the author's statement, "In the world of spirituality, nondualists are the only experts."
5. Do you agree with the idea that "God is both perfectly hidden and perfectly revealed in all things?" Explain your answer.
6. Explain the meaning of Augustine's dictum, "If you understand God, then it is not God."
7. Assess the author's statement that a person's view of God influences his or her view of reality (of life, the cosmos, others, and themselves).
8. What are the advantages and disadvantages of the idea of a "personal God"?
9. Explain the meaning of the term "panentheism," and assess its usefulness in conceptualizing God.
10. Which of Borg's two biblical models for God do you find most attractive, the "monarchical" or the "Spirit" model? Must we choose between them? Is there a better model?
11. Assess the advantages and disadvantages of Tillich's reference to God as Ground of Being.

---

verbally and sacramentally and those who prefer to worship spontaneously and wholeheartedly, with the senses and the emotions.

Chapter 6

Rethinking Scripture

CHRISTIANITY, THE PREDOMINANT, MOST accessible, and most diffuse of the world's religions, has arguably inspired the world's greatest art, music, and architecture. It has also inspired its most memorable speeches, sermons, and lectures; its most elevated theology and philosophy; and its most elegant rhetoric and prose. At the heart of this movement that has captured the imagination of people around the globe is its scripture, known as the Holy Bible, a library of books divided into testaments, one Jewish and the other Christian.

The Sacredness of Scripture

The Bible, the all-time best-selling book, is the most read, best known, most published, and most widely disseminated book in the world. Its value is inestimable, for it has single-handedly changed the course of world history, guiding empires, influencing legal systems, and affecting the lives of untold millions around the globe. Christians have always affirmed a close relationship between the Bible and God, just as other religions affirm a close connection between the sacred and their holy scriptures. Foundational to reading the Bible is a decision about how to view its origin. Is it a divine product, a human product, or somehow both?

For two thousand years the Bible, in part or in whole, has been viewed as sacred by generations of believers. At the time of their composition, however, the books of the Bible were not considered to be part of scripture. Rather, the various parts of the Bible became sacred through canonization, a process that took several centuries. For Christians, the status of the Bible as sacred scripture means it is the primary collection of writings they know, definitive for faith and practice. The sacredness of scripture is validated by its ability to inspire believers in every age, thereby authenticating its enduring message.

Building on the conviction that divine revelation and manmade religion are fundamentally irreconcilable, many Christians believe that the only choice a person can make about the Bible is to view it either as the infallible, inerrant word of God or as a collection of fairy tales with little or no value for modern people. Since the latter is what unbelievers think, fundamentalist Christians believe they must view the Bible as God's very word of truth, defending it in all respects, even on historical and scientific matters. For many, the Bible's reliability is so critical that they will argue, "If I can't believe the Bible when it speaks about creation or history, then how can I believe it about Jesus Christ and salvation?" To frame the question of the inspiration and authority of the Bible in this manner, however, is to do an injustice to the traditional doctrines of the inspiration and authority of scripture.

Acknowledging the obvious human element in the Bible, modern Christians generally take a both/and stance regarding biblical authorship: The Bible is both divine and human. However, this approach is also problematic. Viewing the Bible as both divine and human leaves us two options. One option is to say that it is all divine and all human. That may sound good, but no one maintains such an unworkable tension. The other, more typical option is to attempt to separate the divine parts from the human parts—as if some come from God and others are human. The parts that come from God are then given greater authority. However, who is to say which parts are divine and which human? The Bible does not come with footnotes that say, "This passage reflects the will of God; the next passage does not." Therefore, those who take the entire Bible as divine are consistent, but they might be consistently wrong.

How, for instance, does one understand the Ten Commandments? Most Christians who think of the Bible as both divine and human would say that the commandments come from God. Does that mean that they are equally authoritative? If so, all Christians should worship God on Saturday, since that is the day clearly in mind as the day of worship. There is biblical evidence that the sanctity of the Sabbath was in effect among the Israelites prior to the revelation of the commandments to Moses on Mount Sinai (cf. Exod 16:22–30). And if the Ten Commandments are divinely inspired, why are they written from a male point of view (for instance, they prohibit coveting your neighbor's wife but say nothing about coveting your neighbor's husband)? Furthermore, the commandments against stealing, adultery, murder, bearing false witness, and so forth are simply rules that make it possible for humans to live together in community. Biblical scholarship affirms that the pattern upon which these commandments are based is a treaty pattern devised by the Hittites, a powerful empire that predated Moses and came to an end prior to the time of Moses. Divine genius is not required to come up with rules like these. This is not to say that the Ten Commandments are unimportant, but rather that their origin is human.[1]

Modern scholars view the Bible as the product of two faith communities, each responding uniquely to divine revelation. The Bible, therefore, contains ancient Israel's perceptions and misperceptions, just as it contains the early Christian movement's perceptions and misperceptions. Likewise, the gospels, which record the account of Jesus, reflect not static truths but rather changing theological perspectives. Moreover, these texts are not the words of eyewitnesses, as is often claimed, but were shaped by the events of the second half of the first century, perhaps even more dramatically than by the events of the time in which Jesus actually lived.

All literature invites interpretation; all important literature demands it. This is particularly true of scripture, its truth claims fraught with meaning and therefore open to investigation. In that respect, there is no such thing as a noninterpretive reading of the Bible. Reading the stories of creation or the stories of Jesus' birth literally involves an interpretive decision equally as much as does the decision to read them metaphorically. When we speak of meaning in relation to a biblical text, five levels come to mind: (1) what the divine author intended (while this concern is primary for conservative readers, it applies indirectly to all who read the Bible as scripture); (2) what the human author intended (this concern should be important to all readers, conservative, moderate, and liberal alike); (3) how biblical scholars and theologians interpret a particular passage or verse (their views, both ancient and modern, are readily available in commentaries, handbooks, Study Bibles, and other interpretive aids. While it is important to recognize the bias or perspective of one's resources, those interested in breadth of insight should consult works from

---

1. Borg, *Reading the Bible*, 26–27.

across the denominational and theological spectrum); (4) how leaders in one's church or denomination interpret a particular passage or verse; and finally, (5) what the text means to you. While this final level is indispensable, we should not arrive at it quickly. Without the corrective of the other levels, this approach to the Bible can result in as many meanings as it has readers.

Scripture as (Internal and External) Dialogue

Humans are meaning-seeking creatures. Without some pattern or significance in their lives, humans fall easily into depression or despair. Language plays a vital role in our quest for meaning, helping us to communicate with others, certainly, but also enabling us to clarify our inner world. In this respect, language gives voice to our feelings, hopes, points of view, and values, as well as giving expression to our personality and identity.

All this gives rise to literature, to wondrous writings such as epics, poems, stories, and historical narrative. Each of these forms of literature are found in the Bible, considered scripture by Jews, Christians, and to some extent Muslims, the three monotheistic faiths also known as the Abrahamic traditions. While Jews, Christians, and Muslims might disagree on the number of books in the Bible and on how to interpret certain passages of scripture, ultimately they are most divided on the individual doctrines formulated from them. When divisive doctrines are set aside and understood in less sectarian ways, Jews, Christians, Muslims, and other people of faith find much commonality in scripture. Our goal in this book is to do just that, to set aside secondary and divisive interpretations of biblical teachings and find their inner commonalities. In so doing, we will discover what readers have always encountered in these writings, a presence that serves as a vehicle or bridge to a transcendent dimension.

For some time now, scripture has gained a bad name. Think only of how the Bible was used in the American South to justify slavery; or how the Old Testament was used by Afrikaners in South Africa to justify apartheid; or how the world's scriptures are used the world over to justify social caste and gender segregation. Secular opponents of religion claim that scripture breeds violence, sectarianism, and intolerance; that it prevents people from thinking for themselves; leads to prejudice between races, cultures, nations, and religions; and encourages delusion. Racists, terrorists, and bigots use scripture to justify prejudice, supremacy, and physical atrocities; fundamentalists and other religious purists campaign against the teaching of evolutionary theory because it contradicts a literal reading of the biblical creation story. If religion preaches compassion, why is there so much hatred between people of different faiths? The answer is clear: scripture has become something it was not intended to be. Is it possible to be a believer today when science and rationality have undermined so many biblical teachings?

Because scripture and theology and beliefs based on the Bible have become such explosive issues, it is important to be clear what scripture is and what it is not. For example, it is crucial to note that an exclusively literal interpretation of the Bible is a recent development. Until the nineteenth century, few people imagined that the first chapter of Genesis was a factual account of the origins of life. For centuries, Jews and Christians maintained highly allegorical and inventive ways of reading and understanding scripture, insisting that a wholly literal reading of the Bible was neither possible nor desirable.

The Jewish scriptures and the New Testament both began as oral proclamations, and throughout history, even long after they were committed to writing, there remained a bias against the written word. In the beginning, scriptures were heard in a communal and ritualistic setting; they were not intended for private use or personal study. Such hearers saw scripture as something to approach intuitively rather than rationally. From that beginning, people feared that a written scripture would encourage inflexibility and serve as a mere wooden code. Documents became scripture not, initially, because they were thought to be divinely inspired, but because they provided a sense of community and identity, bringing people together rather than dividing them into sects and denominations. When people approached the Bible intuitively, they found it produced a holistic understanding of reality in which things that seemed separate and even opposite coincided and revealed an unexpected unity, a sense of completeness and oneness.

Scripture is best understood as dialogue, its meaning not limited to what particular individuals say it is, be they religious authorities or scholarly experts. The point of this dialogue is that each reader must interact with the text, personalizing it. The following questions, then, are central to each reading: What do I see in the text? How does a text speak in a given existential moment? In this interaction, we must be careful not to freeze the meaning of a text, thereby reducing it to "dead orthodoxy." What is of ultimate importance, however, is not the text itself, but that it serve as a vehicle or bridge to transcendence, rending readers more loving, compassionate, and caring for their planet and for all of its creatures, great and small.

A Canon within the Canon

For centuries, primal peoples and then Hindus, Buddhists, and eventually Jews, Christians, and Muslims, understood religion as a spiritual discipline. They read their scriptures less as something to be read intellectually and explored exclusively with their minds, but rather as a spiritual process that opened them to transcendence. Because it is necessary for people living in modern multicultural and interreligious societies to read the Bible with an open, progressive, and questioning faith, I suggest that they construct a "canon within the canon," that is, that they look for a biblical concept that is essential for all time.

Fortunately, others have preceded us in that quest. For example, when Jesus was asked to summarize biblical teaching, he pointed to the Golden Rule ("Do unto others as you would have them do unto you") and to the Great Commandment ("Love the Lord your God with all your ability and your neighbor as yourself"). Likewise, the early Christian teacher Paul of Tarsus summarized biblical teaching with the "principle of charity" ("the greatest of all values and ideals is love"), as did the great Christian theologian Augustine of Hippo, who claimed that scripture teaches nothing but love. Rabbi Hillel, a contemporary of Jesus, once summarized the entire Torah (the revealed will of God) with the words: "What is hateful to yourself, do not do to your fellow man. That is the whole of the Torah. The rest is commentary."

When people are attuned, awake, and responsive, reality is often "unveiled" for them, and they are able to hear, see, and understand aspects of their belief system at odds with long-held assumptions. In many cases, people of faith—Christian or otherwise—often become so familiar with the "story" of their faith that a veil is pulled over their eyes, making them unable to experience its transformative power.

Perhaps the most deadening aspect of Christianity is that Christians live with twenty-twenty hindsight. They know the story. They know the plot—how it begins and ends—and who the winners are. However, we are living now at a time of religious change and transformation some would call a paradigm shift. Perhaps there hasn't been an opportunity before for people of faith to open up the core questions again and to ask: What does it mean to believe in God? What do we mean by Christianity? What is the faith filter through which we view truth and reality? What is the lens by which we read and interpret scripture? What do we mean when we profess belief in creation or incarnation? Who is this Master that Christians profess as Lord and Savior?

A Tale of Two Paradigms

It is no secret that we are living in a time of major change, resulting in monumental religious conflict, chiefly in North American mainline denominations. While there are many ways of being Christian in our day, two paradigms—two overarching interpretive frameworks—may be helpful to describe the current conflict in Christianity. The first, the Precritical Paradigm, has been a common form of Christianity for the past several hundred years. This approach should not be associated with Christianity as a whole, though it remains a major voice, perhaps the majority voice in global Christianity. Its adherents

1. View the Bible as a divine product, as the unique revelation of God.
2. Interpret the Bible literally.
3. Equate faith with belief; the Christian life centered in believing now for the sake of salvation.
4. View the afterlife as central; the Christian life being about requirements and rewards, with the main reward a blessed afterlife.
5. View Christianity as the only true religion, and belief in God, the Bible, and Jesus as the way to heaven.

This paradigm should not be equated with "the Christian tradition," as though it were the dominant or only way of being Christian throughout history. In actuality it is the product of modernity, shaped by the birth of modern science and scientific ways of knowing. Since the Enlightenment of the seventeenth century, modernity has questioned both the divine origin and the literal-factual truth of many parts of the Bible, and the Precritical Paradigm is a response to that modern critique.

A second way of seeing Christianity, the Postcritical Paradigm, has been in existence for over a hundred years and has become an increasingly attractive movement within mainline Protestant denominations and in the Catholic Church. Like the earlier paradigm, its central features are a response to the Enlightenment, only in this case it embraces many Enlightenment ideals, including an appreciation of science, historical scholarship, religious pluralism, and cultural diversity. It also arose out of awareness of how Christianity had contributed to racism, sexism, nationalism, exclusivism, and other harmful ideologies. Its adherents

1. View the Bible as a human response to God.
2. Interpret the Bible historically and metaphorically.
3. View faith relationally rather than dogmatically—faith being the way of the heart, not the way of the head.
4. View the Christian life as one of relationship and transformation. Being Christian is not about meeting requirements for a future reward in an afterlife, and not very much about believing. Rather, the Christian life is about a relationship with God that transforms life in the present.
5. Affirm religious pluralism. This paradigm considers Christianity as one of the world's great enduring religions, as a particular response to the experience of God in our Western cultural stream.

From the perspective of the Postcritical Paradigm, the Precritical Paradigm seems anti-intellectual and rigidly (but selectively) moralistic. Its insistence on biblical literalism seems inadequate, as does its rejection of science whenever it conflicts with literalism. It seems to emphasize individual purity more than compassion and justice. And its exclusivism, its rejection of other religions as inadequate or worse, is objectionable. Can it be that God is known in only one religion—and perhaps only in the "right" form of that religion?[2]

The Postcritical Paradigm, guided by the holistic possibilities found in the dialectical model, places equal importance upon faith (as displayed in religious beliefs and practices, both corporate and private) and reason (as displayed in the disciplines of philosophy, science, religious studies, and other academic subjects) in the quest for knowledge and understanding of reality. It also values the antithetical anthropological perspectives suggested in the opening chapters of the book of Genesis—humans are made "in the image of God" in the first creation account (Genesis 1) and "from the dust of the ground" in the second creation account (Genesis

---

2. Borg, *Heart of Christianity*, 16.

2)—and the tension created by these competing yet harmonizable views. Dialectical thought is simultaneously God-affirming and world affirming. Advocates of the Postcritical Paradigm need not choose, indeed should not choose, one over the other.

The Bible in the Postcritical Paradigm

The Bible represents the heart of the Christian tradition, providing Christians their identity, their sacred story. Despite its formational nature, the Bible has become a stumbling block for many Christians today. In particular, many are leaving the church because the Precritical Paradigm's way of reading the Bible—with its emphasis on biblical infallibility, historical factuality, and moral and doctrinal absolutes—ceases to make sense to them.

The Postcritical Paradigm provides an alternative to biblical literalism. Utilizing three adjectives—*historical, metaphorical,* and *sacramental*—it describes how scripture should be understood. These three approaches apply as well to the creeds and other normative Christian teachings.[3]

1. To speak of *the Bible as a historical product* is to see that it is a human product, not a divine product. Not "absolute truth" but relatively and culturally conditioned, the Bible uses the language and concepts of the cultures in which it took shape. It tells us how our spiritual ancestors saw things, not how God sees things. The Bible is not verbally inspired, since the emphasis is not upon words inspired by God but on people moved by their experience of God.

For the Postcritical Paradigm, describing the Bible as sacred scripture and therefore as "holy" is to value the historical process known as canonization. The documents that make up the Bible were not "sacred" when they were written, but over time were declared sacred, meaning that they became the most important documents for that community, providing its foundation and shaping its identity.

2. Much of the language of the Bible is metaphorical: one-third of the Old Testament is poetry or semi-poetical literature. To speak of *the Bible as metaphor* is to emphasize that this language should not be interpreted literally. Metaphor does not mean that the Bible is not true, but rather that it is not primarily concerned with facticity. The Bible does contain

3. The following points are adapted from Borg, *Heart of Christianity*, 43–60.

history, but even when a text contains historical memory, its meaning is more than (not less than) literal. For example, although the exile in Babylon in the sixth century BCE really happened, the way the story is told gives it a more than historical meaning. It becomes a metaphorical narrative of exile and return, providing images of the human condition and its remedy. In other cases, as the Genesis stories of creation, there may be little or no historical factuality. Though these stories are not literally factual, they are profoundly true.

Because the gospels combine memory and metaphor, some of these accounts, when literalized, become literally incredible. The story of Jesus changing water into wine at the wedding in Cana (John 2:1–11) illustrates the point. A literal reading of the story emphasizes the spectacular event as a sign of Jesus's identity, "proof" that he was divine. A metaphorical reading of this story yields a different meaning. It notes the story's literary context in John's gospel as the opening scene of the public activity of Jesus. It seems to be John's way of saying: "Here in a nutshell is what the story of Jesus is about."

The story begins: "On the third day, there was a wedding." The phrase "on the third day" evokes the Easter story at the end of the gospel. The imagery of a wedding banquet helps us view the ministry of Jesus as a celebration at which the wine never runs out and the best is saved for last. Here we have a pointer to the sacramental nature of the Christian life and to the belief that Jesus is God's best.

A metaphorical reading of the gospels provides rich meaning for Christians in all times and places; a literal reading misses all of this, emphasizing belief in the miraculous elements rather than on its meaning for a life of faith. Metaphorical language is *a way of seeing*. To apply this to the Bible means that in addition to its metaphorical language and metaphorical narratives, the Bible as a whole may be thought of as a "giant" metaphor. "Thus the point is not to believe in the Bible—but to see our lives with God through it."[4]

3. To speak of *the Bible as sacrament* is to say that it mediates the sacred. If a sacrament is a physical vehicle or vessel for the Spirit, the Bible is sacrament in the sense that it is a visible human product whereby God becomes present to us.

For the Postcritical Paradigm, "the Bible—human in origin, sacred in status and function—is both metaphor and sacrament. As metaphor, it

---

4. Borg, *Heart of Christianity*, 57.

is a way of seeing—a way of seeing God and our life with God. As sacrament, it is a way that God speaks to us and comes to us."[5] The Bible is a two-way bridge, a path to the divine and a way to connect to our deepest self. Like a backboard in the game of basketball, scripture is a means to an end, not an end in itself.

The Bible and Faith Formation

People read the Bible for many reasons: literarily (as great literature), philosophically (as a guide for moral and reflective thought), theologically (as a compendium of truth), or devotionally (as a resource for meditation and a source of comfort). Despite the Bible's widespread scriptural use, most devout people read it only occasionally, and superficially. How people read it is perhaps more important than why they read it. For those who wish to engage with scripture seriously and in depth, I recommend that you find a method of study that works for you, whether individually or with others, and commit to it. Of many valid ways of reading scripture, the following are recommended:

- Reading for *information*—to learn as much as possible about the setting of the authors and their primary audience in order to discover the original meaning of a particular passage of scripture and its potential application.

- Reading for *formation*—to establish one's identity, values, and beliefs in order to live meaningfully, joyously, and securely.

- Reading for *transformation*—to provide resources for developing soulcentrically rather than egocentrically, aligning more deeply with one's powers of nurturing and creating, presence and wonder.

Of course, it is quite possible for these approaches to overlap, due to the complexity of our intellectual, theological, and spiritual needs. It is equally possible that biblical passages convey messages appropriate to our varied abilities and needs. Scripture is multivalent, meaning that it's message allows for multiple interpretations. While one text might strike terror in the heart of an unrepentant person, the same passage might exhort devout believers to greater faithfulness and even greater freedom. When you read any book or section of the Bible, particularly in a group setting, keep in mind the possibility that biblical passages contain

5. Borg, *Heart of Christianity*, 59.

multiple messages, depending on one's needs, temperament, and spiritual journey. Scripture, like a good smorgasbord, provides healthy options for different appetites. And you don't always have to eat the same food; sometimes a change of diet can be helpful.

As Paul showed in 1 Corinthians, the important thing is to keep growing spiritually. Paul's concern with the Corinthians was that they were in a state of spiritual immaturity, unable to eat solid food. It takes time—and conscious effort—to grow spiritually, from egocentrism to soulcentrism. How people hear and read scripture (eat spiritually) reflects their spiritual maturity.

In chapter 2, we defined a cult as a sect, group, or movement that affirms it alone has the truth. In some cases, most Christianity-based cults develop their own do-it-yourself theology, based on new revelation, viewed as an extra-biblical source of authority, equaling or superseding the Bible. In some cases, cults may not rely on additional scripture, relying instead on obscure verses or unique interpretations of familiar passages. Such cults can be defined as "a group of people polarized over someone's interpretation of the Bible."

Interestingly, viewing faith as a never-ending process of formation can set us free from manipulative and dehumanizing cultic thinking. As people grow spiritually, psychologically, emotionally, and intellectually, they develop new ways of thinking and living, ways that challenge stagnant and polarized ways of interpreting scripture. Having already introduced three ways of reading scripture—for information, formation, and transformation—I now correlate these concepts with the four stages of faith formation.

Unlike a ladder, which one climbs rung by rung, faith formation adds new dimensions to what one already is, like a tree adds rings. Hence, formation is central to each stage of faith, the scaffolding for growth. The following terms suggest biblical roles for each stage of faith formation. Like the stages of faith, they are fluid and dynamic in nature, regularly overlapping. Nevertheless, they indicate the central task or role of scripture for each stage:

1. Stage One—foundation
2. Stage Two—information
3. Stage Three—liberation
4. Stage Four—transformation

Interestingly, certain books or portions of scripture seem particularly relevant to the task of a particular stage. For example, the books of Genesis, Deuteronomy, Proverbs, the gospel of Mark, the pastoral epistles (1 and 2 Timothy and Titus), and the epistles of Hebrews and James might work well for Stage One Christians. The historical books of Exodus, Joshua, 1 and 2 Samuel, and 1 and 2 Kings in the Old Testament and the gospel of Matthew, the book of Acts, the epistles of 1 Corinthians, 1Thessalonians, Philippians, and 1 and 2 Peter might be appropriate for Stage Two Christians, while the Old Testament books of Psalms, Job, and Ecclesiastes might be appropriate to Stage Three Christians, and from the New Testament, the gospel of Luke.[6]

Nevertheless, for Stage Four Christians, each book becomes more intriguing and inspiring, and, of course, Jesus looks more brilliant than ever in Stage Four. He seems radiantly different from the Jesus of Stage One and Stage Two preachers, who seem stuck in orthodoxy, resisting the implications of his radical message.

Core Teachings of the Bible

In my upper level class "Global Christianity," generally filled with students minoring in Religious Studies, I ask students to complete an assignment in which they are told to reduce the biblical message to its core principle. As you might imagine, the answers I receive vary greatly, as students focus on their own beliefs and spiritual experiences. Since I would not ask students to answer questions I have not previously wrestled with myself, here is my answer. At the heart of scripture are two central teachings, foundational to Christian faith:

1. The theological core—the existence of a Creator God, whose essence is love, and

2. The anthropological core—that all human beings are made in God's image, meaning that they are capable and responsible to live in love, to enjoy intimacy with God, and to share God's love with all creation.

As key biblical passages indicate, love for God and one's neighbor are core teachings of the Bible. When Jesus was asked to summarize the

---

6. For suggestions on reading the Bible as a narrative in faith formation, see appendix A, "The Unfolding Drama of Faith in the Biblical Storyline."

commandments, he responded without hesitation that this involved loving God with our whole being and loving our neighbor as ourselves (Matt 22:36–40). In Luke's version (Luke 10:25–28), Jesus tells a parable that makes it clear that one's neighbor includes the stranger, the outsider, the outcast, and the unclean. In the Sermon on the Mount, Jesus' classic exposition of ethical teachings, Jesus teaches a way of life that culminates in a call to love the enemy (Matt 5:43). According to Jesus, humans need to love as God loves, with non-discriminatory love.

If that weren't revolutionary enough, we could turn to Paul, the originator of the phrase "faith working through love" (Gal 5:6). When he summarizes what God requires and desires, Paul says nothing about correct belief. Rather, he declares, "For the whole law is summed up in a single commandment, 'You shall love your neighbor as yourself.'" (Gal 5:14). When the author of the epistle of James summarizes the religious task, he states simply, "Religion that is pure and undefiled before God, the Father, is this: to care for orphans and widows in their distress" (1:27). What matters to James centers in caring for people, not confessing beliefs. That is why he goes on to say, "faith without works is dead." Real faith is found not simply in words that express compliance, but in actions that express care. We find the same in the epistles of John. In John 4:7–12, John tells us that "love is from God . . . . for God is love." Then, echoing Jesus' words about the greatest commandment, John continues, "those who do not love a brother or sister whom they have seen, cannot love God whom they have not seen. The commandment we have from him is this: those who love God must love their brothers and sisters also" (1 John 4:20–21).

This emphasis on love is not unique to the Christian scriptures. When Jesus spoke of the great commandment, he was quoting from Deuteronomy 6:5, a text central to Jewish liturgy and life, and from Leviticus 19:18. In Proverbs 17:5 and 19:17, for example, Jews are called to make love central, for the way one treats the poor is the way one treats God. The prophet Hosea echoes this emphasis when he proclaims that God desires compassion, not sacrifice (6:6). Similar teachings are found in the Qur'an and are central to Hinduism, Buddhism, and Sikhism as well.

When Christians think of world religions, they usually think of differences in belief and practice. The deeper question, however, is not whether you are Christian, Buddhist, or atheist, but rather, what kind of Christian, Buddhist, or atheist are you? Are you a believer who puts your distinct beliefs first, or are you a person of faith who puts love first? Are you a believer whose beliefs put you in competition and conflict with people of differing beliefs, or are you a person of faith whose faith moves you toward others with love?

As we have been saying, faith develops organically, not by progressing through stages but by adding new dimensions to older ones. Like a ring on a tree, each new sage includes the previous stage as it transcends it. Thus, a key function of families and communities of faith is to help younger members develop the sequential capacity for dualistic thinking (in Simplicity), pragmatic thinking (in Complexity), critical thinking (in Perplexity), and non-dual seeing (in Clarity). However, in addition to being cumulative, the stages are iterative. After you are in Clarity for a while, Clarity becomes your new Simplicity. And if you live long enough, you will surely face new levels of Complexity, which will lead to a new season of Perplexity, and so on. However, after you cycle through the four stages a few times, you begin to feel that dualism, pragmatism, relativism, and nondual holism have simply become four ways of seeing or four skill sets at your disposal. After a few runs around the spiral, you become less conscious of being "in" only one stage, and instead, you feel you constantly experience all of them. At any point, you can access all the strengths of these stages and fall for any of their temptations.

As learners and seekers develop through the stages of faith, it is imperative that the core teachings of the Bible—particularly that God is love and that humans are to reflect that love—be introduced initially and regularly. Such passages should include 1 Corinthians 13, Matthew 22:36-40, Romans 13:8-10, Galatians 5:1-26, 1 John 4:7-21, and parables of Jesus such as the Parable of the Good Samaritan (Luke 10:25-37) and teachings such as love of enemies in Matthew 5:43.

Ecclesiastes: A Book for All Seasons

Because of its honesty, the book of Ecclesiastes is recommended reading for all seasons and stages of life. Like Proverbs, Ecclesiastes is a collection of disparate items, including maxims, aphorisms, and admonitions. Lying somewhere between a treatise and a collection of sayings, the book alternates sayings and admonitions with lengthier meditations. Many Christians find the biblical book of Ecclesiastes perplexing. Why is it in the Bible? they wonder. How can a book whose thesis expresses "vanity" or "futility" in life be consistent with faith in God and a moral order in the universe? For Qoheleth, the author of Ecclesiastes, life without justice and fairness, without just reward and punishment, seems meaningless and absurd.

As we learn from Israel's wisdom literature, the qualities that constitute "wisdom" are accessible in three primary forms: wisdom taught by God, wisdom taught by nature, and wisdom that arises from reflection on human experience. In the case of Qoheleth, he came to his conclusions existentially, through experience and by experimentation. In speaking of his quest for the meaning of life, Qoheleth focuses on several candidates: knowledge, pleasure, power, wealth, love, and life itself. He presents evidence for rejecting each of these as adequate and remains skeptical about easy answers. After a lifetime of investigation, he concludes that life is nothing more than a meaningful series of unrelated events. The task of wisdom, as Qoheleth sees it, is to clarify its own limits, to understand what can and what cannot be known. Qoheleth's answer to the questions he raises is not nihilism, however. He does not wish to deny God's presence or influence, but rather to emphasize the limits of human wisdom. Hence the famous theme: "Vanity of vanities," which means that humans cannot know with finality what they wish to know.

Considering Qoheleth to be a philosopher, Peter Kreeft (Professor of Philosophy at Boston University) labels Ecclesiastes the greatest of all books of philosophy. Kreeft does not base his assessment on the book's logical argumentation, since the author frequently rambles, changes his mind, and even allows his moods to rule his thinking. He does not consider Ecclesiastes great because of its thesis, for how can a book about meaninglessness be meaningful? Rather, Ecclesiastes is great because it is profoundly honest. Vanity and meaninglessness cannot detect themselves; it takes wisdom to know vanity, and profundity to know meaninglessness. For Kreeft, Ecclesiastes is also great because it poses life's most important ethical question, the question of the *summum bonum* (the greatest good, highest value, or ultimate end of meaning of life).

Kreeft examines Qoheleth's message under the concept of "toil," by which he means not simply "work" but all human pursuits. Qoheleth experiments with five toils, valued universally as worthy aims of life, evaluating each as a candidate for life's *summum bonum*. They are:

1. wisdom (philosophy to fill the mind), cf. 1:12–18;

2. pleasure (hedonism to fill the body), cf. 2:1–11;

3. wealth and power (materialism to fill the wallet), cf. 5:8—6:6; 2:8;

4. duty and altruism (ethics to fill the conscience), cf. 4:9–11;

5. conventional religion (religion to fill the spirit), cf. 5:1–7; 7:16b.

Qoheleth tried all five ways and found them lacking in meaning and unable to produce happiness. His approach is not argumentative, but experimental. He lives five lives and shares the result of his experience. In the end, all five candidates for life's *summum bonum*, all endeavors in which humans place hope and to which they give allegiance, prove futile. The reason for their futility, according to Kreeft, is that they are infected by the five "vanities," each of which can kill meaning. The five vanities are:

1. human endeavors as vain and indifferent (9:1–2, 11);

2. death as the certain and final end of life (3:19–21);

3. time as a boring repetitive cycle (3:1–15);

4. evil as a perennial and unsolvable problem (8:14; 3:16; 4:1);

5. God as an unknowable mystery (8:17; 11:5).

Since most humans disagree with Qoheleth's supposition that "all is vanity," they use three approaches—psychology, philosophy, and conventional religion—to circumvent his conclusion, but according to Qoheleth, all are invalid. Kreeft disagrees, finding benefit in all three, but he relies on a fourth—revelation—to provide final answers. Considering Ecclesiastes to be divinely revealed, Kreeft argues that God is using a kind of "Socratic method" here, raising questions and providing challenges that believers must answer with the help of scripture. The Bible, Kreeft suggests, is a diptych, a two-paneled picture. Ecclesiastes represents the first panel, the question. The rest of the Bible is the second panel, the answer. Kreeft uses an image from the historian Arnold Toynbee, that history is "challenge and response." Ecclesiastes is the challenge; the remainder of scripture is the response. Kreeft concludes, "Ecclesiastes is the question to which Christ is the answer."[7]

As a philosopher, Kreeft argues that the question of the *summum bonum* is raised only by existentialist philosophers today, and the answer they give sounds much like Qoheleth's motto: life is meaningless, vain, and absurd. When we explore Qoheleth's axiom, we must be aware that he is not speaking from a "faith perspective" (such as Job's conclusion in

---

7. Kreeft, *Three Philosophies*, 56. Kreeft's discussion on the five toils and the five vanities is taken from pages 35–53. His view of scripture, naïve by modern standards, nevertheless bears consideration.

42:5–6), but rather is addressing "the surface of life" (perhaps this phrase captures best the meaning of Qoheleth's "under the sun"). Ecclesiastes is brutally honest, "the truest picture of the surface that has ever been written."[8] An answer is meaningless without its question, and perhaps the purpose of Ecclesiastes in the Bible is to raise life's existential questions.

Kreeft views Qoheleth as more a philosopher than a theologian, claiming that God is only an object in Ecclesiastes, never the subject.[9] While Kreeft's position is debatable (particularly his definition of "philosophy" as humans searching for God and his understanding of "theology" as verbal revelation), Kreeft proceeds to a stunning observation: Ecclesiastes is revelation precisely in being the absence of divine revelation, revelation by darkness rather than by light. Kreeft quotes Kierkegaard: "If I could prescribe just one remedy for all the ills of the modern world, I would prescribe silence."[10] Ecclesiastes creates silence, and out of that darkness God reveals what life is like when God does not reveal to us life's meaning. For Kreeft, Ecclesiastes frames the Bible as death frames life.

While Ecclesiastes can be said to be a book for all the seasons of faith, it can serve as a source of great comfort to those in Perplexity. The fact that there is room in the Bible for a book of questions and doubts means that there should be room in the community of faith for people full of their own questions and doubts.

Questions for Discussion and Reflection

1. In your estimation, why should we read the Bible? Does our motivation matter?

2. What do Christians generally mean when they say that the Bible is "holy"? Does the word "sacred" necessarily imply anything supernatural about the origin or nature of scripture? Explain your answer.

3. What does the author mean by "dead orthodoxy"? If we should not read scripture primarily for its doctrinal teachings, what should our primary purpose be?

---

8. Kreeft, *Three Philosophies*, 19.

9. Biblical scholars have been intrigued by the presence of Ecclesiastes in the Hebrew canon, since the book lacks divine speech, meaning that God is never quoted as speaking directly.

10. Kreeft, *Three Philosophies*, 31.

4. What is your "canon within a canon"? Explain your answer.

5. In this chapter, the author lists five levels of meaning inherent in a biblical text. When you read the Bible, which level or levels are most important? Explain your asnwer.

6. In your estimation, what is the fundamental difference between the Precritical and the Postcritical paradigms? Which of these best reflects your perspective? Why?

7. Utilizing the three adjectives implicit in the Postcritical Paradigm's approach to scripture, which one best captures your understanding and view of the Bible? Explain your answer.

8. In this chapter, the author names three (or possibly four) ways of reading scripture. Which of these best describes your reasons for reading the Bible? Explain your answer.

9. In your estimation, what are the core teachings of the Bible? (If possible, limit your list to five or less).

10. After reading the segment on the book of Ecclesiastes, what for you is life's *summum bonum*? Explain your answer.

Chapter 7

Rethinking Creation Theology

PERHAPS YOU HAVE HEARD the saying, "All I really need to know I learned in kindergarten." This quote, the title of a 1989 book written by Robert Fulghum, indicates that all we need to know about how to live, act, and relate to others, we learned (or should have learned) at an early age, no later than the start of our formal education in kindergarten. As children, we learned (or knew intuitively) that imagination is stronger than knowledge, that myth is more potent than history, that dreams are more powerful than facts, and that persons are more valuable than things.

The same, I suggest, is true of religion, theology, and spirituality. All we really need to know about these things we find in Genesis 1. While it might come as a surprise to many readers, Genesis 1 was not the first chapter or passage of the Bible inspired, written, or composed. Actually, it was recorded rather late—long after Genesis 2 and 3. Nevertheless, Genesis 1 is rightly placed first in the Bible, not only because it provides an account of creation, that is, of beginnings, but because it contains all we really need to know about religion, all that is foundational to spirituality.

The Biblical Doctrine of Creation

The biblical account of creation is found in Genesis 1–3. Having studied these chapters over a lifetime, rethinking and reviewing their popular and familiar interpretations, recently I arrived at a new realization about the opening chapter of the Bible: Genesis 1 is not simply about human beginnings or even about the beginning of the Jewish (and Christian) religion. In fact, it is not simply about monotheism or the role of divine sovereignty in creation. It can also be read—perhaps even best read—as the origin and nature of a universal spirituality.

Examined literarily, Genesis 1–3 narrates two stories (Genesis 1:1–2:4a, called the Priestly or P account, and Genesis 2:4b–3:24, called the Yahwist or J account) in tension with one another and contradictory when read cognitively, rationally, or literally. However, when read spiritually, creatively, and imaginatively, each account expands our understanding of reality. Genesis 1, in particular, beckons us to experience the primal wholeness, a purposeful and meaningful reality in which all is good, its goodness guaranteed by a loving and benevolent creator God.

The Priestly story of creation (Gen. 1:1–2:4a) and the Yahwist story of the Fall (Gen. 3:1–24) were intended to be read aloud or heard to be appreciated. The original setting of these passages, widely gleaned in modern times for historical and scientific truths, is not a laboratory or a classroom but rather corporate worship. The setting of creation-faith within worship is clearly evident in Psalm 24, a three-part liturgy once used during great pilgrimage festivals celebrating Yahweh's kingship. This psalm was undoubtedly used originally in connection with a processional bearing of the Ark of the Covenant into Jerusalem. The opening word of the psalm, which announce that Yahweh is creator, functioned as an introit: "The earth is the Lord's and all that is in it, the world, and those who live in it; for he has founded it on the seas, and established it on the rivers" (24:1–2). The second part, in question-and-response format (24:3–6), is a liturgy for admission to the temple, and the third, an "entrance liturgy" (24:7–10), was sung antiphonally in the presence of the ark, understood to be Yahweh's throne-seat. In this liturgical setting, the function of creation language is to set the stage for praising God. Thus, in the book of Psalms, known as the hymnbook of Judaism, the affirmation that God is the creator is a call to worship.

The word "creation" is neither scientific or philosophical; rather it is theological, a language whose affirmations should not be confused with statements made in the context of secular or scientific thought. In the Bible, the announcement that God is the creator primarily concerns the source and basis of life's meaning. Negatively, it counters the notion that the world is at our disposal, to use or misuse as we please. To understand the creation stories at the beginning of the Bible, we ought to divest our minds of scientific and philosophical preconceptions and begin with the Psalms, which praise God as the creator. While the position of the

Priestly story of creation is the opening of a cosmic drama, the prelude of the story of God's special dealings with humanity, the form of the story suggests that it was shaped by liturgical usage over a period of many generations, perhaps in connection with one of the great pilgrimage festivals of Israel, and thus it is told confessionally to glorify the God of Israel.

This leads to an important point. When creation-faith is interpreted within the context of worship, there is a tendency to shift the accent from creation as the event at the beginning to a relationship in the present, from the horizontal dimension (the movement of events from beginning to end) to the vertical dimension (the relationship between God and humanity). In our time, the existentialist interpretation of creation has found wide support. In his commentary on Genesis 1–11, Alan Richardson suggests that we consider these stories as "parables," to be read as poetry, not prose. The parables of Genesis, he says, contain a special kind of truth: "not the truth with which history and geography, astronomy and geology, deal; it is not the literal truth of the actual observation of measurable things and events; it is ultimate truth, the truth which can be grasped only by the imagination, and which can be expressed by image and symbolism."[1] Such truth, "the truth of religious awareness," cannot be expressed in philosophical, theological, or psychological terms, for that would be to depersonalize it. You are Adam, I am Eve; this is our story!

Psalm 8, related to the Priestly creation account in Genesis 1, is an eloquent witness to the meaning of creation-faith in the liturgy of Israel's worship. This hymn begins and ends with an exclamation of praise to God's glory and majesty, which, to the eye of faith, are evident in nature. The psalmist knows that we sometimes take this world for granted, and yet he knows too that praise is the sign that we are alive, that we are fully human. Creation-faith focuses upon the relationship between God and humanity: "When I look at your heavens, the work of your fingers, the moon and the stars that you have established, what are human beings that you are mindful of them, mortals that you care for them?" (Ps 8:3–4). It is not simply that humans, in contrast to God, are finite. As the book of Ecclesiastes shows, the awareness of the gulf fixed between creature and creator can prompt a feeling of futility and desolation (Eccl 1:12–14; 3:16–22; 6:1–2). Rather, creation-faith provides context for understanding existence, the awareness that our relationship with God is one of

---

1. Richardson, *Genesis I–XI*, 30.

incomprehensible grace. As we see also in the Priestly creation story, where humans are said to be created "in the image of God" (Gen 1:27), praise rises to a climax as the psalmist draws upon the old liturgical tradition: "You have made [humans] a little lower than God, and crowned them with glory and honor. You have given them dominion over the works of your hands; you have put all things under their feet" (Ps 8:5–6).

In the Bible, creation reveals wisdom through its patterns. Creation passages such as those found in Genesis (see 1:1–2:4a), the Psalms (see 8:1–9; 24:1–2), Proverbs (see 8:22–36) and in the prologue to John's gospel (see 1:1–5) dare us to believe that the universe runs by the logic of creativity, goodness, and love. The universe is God's creative project, filled with beauty, opportunity, challenge, and meaning. It runs on the meaning or pattern we see in the Pentateuch and as embodied in the life of Jesus, by which humans are enjoined to love God and neighbor as oneself. In the life of the Christ, as in creation, pregnancy abounds; goodness multiplies; freedom grows; meaning expands; wisdom flows; healing happens; and goodness flows freely.

What, then, are the life lessons found in Genesis 1? The following list, while not exhaustive, includes the five pillars of all unifying and transformative faith:

1. *The existence of God.* In their thinking and living, people of religious faith always assume or presuppose God. Knowing that God's existence can neither be proven nor disproven, they simply think and live out of the divine reality. They assume that God is knowable (that is, can be experienced), even though such "knowledge" is unlike all other knowing. While we know we cannot understand God cognitively or fully, our conception or idea of God is crucial, for how we view or understand God shapes and influences how we view and treat others, ourselves, and all other living things in nature.

2. *The goodness of creation.* The book of Genesis is traditionally read as a book of history. Its name, "Genesis," meaning "origin," refers generally to the origin of humanity and to the beginning of all human history. In its literary context, Genesis is designed specifically to serve as the prologue to the history of Israel. The main purpose of Genesis 1, however, is neither historical, intellectual, or scientific, but theological and religious. In that respect, there are three general functions of the creation account. (1) Negatively, it is antipolytheistic and anti-idolatrous. (2) Positively, it teaches about God's nature

as Creator. (3) Practically, it teaches that God is loving, benevolent, and good, meaning that life is purposeful and good when humans live responsibly with nature, God, and others.

3. *The value, dignity, and equality of all human beings.* Because all humans are made in God's image, all are good by nature. The universality of this image implies that all are equal in value and in dignity. Because God loves all people equally, humans should not discriminate by gender, race, class, creed, or nationality. Because all humans are capable of knowing and relating to God equally, all are to honor and respect one another fully, freely, and authentically.

4. *All things are interrelated.* In Genesis, humans are given the role of co-workers with God, stewards and caregivers of God's creation. Because there is an organic connection between all things, all religions, nations, peoples, animals, and plants are connected and interdependent. As we read in Ecclesiastes 3:1, for everything there is a purpose.

5. *The unfolding of continuous creation.* While Genesis 1 describes creation to have come into existence by fiat, that is, as spoken into existence by God, the underlying reality is that all things emerge organically and develop from within, darkness leading to light; light to water and air; water and air to earth and seas; earth and seas to vegetation; vegetation to living creatures; living creatures to fish, birds, and animals of the earth; and out of the animals, humankind. Thus formed and shaped—one reality and one creature from the other—this creation continues to evolve, according to a pattern, destiny, and purpose known only to the Creator. As understood by theologians such as Augustine of Hippo, the Creator endowed the universe, from its opening moments, with the potential for evolving toward the kind of complexity we see in the cell and in genetic DNA. Having done so, the universe unfolds according to an internal capacity for self-organization that removes the need for ongoing divine manipulation. This self-organizing universe may be seen as continuously moving through a "field of promise," consisting of all the possibilities offered at the start. In some sense, God (or "the Spirit of God") is this field of promise.

Despite all this cosmic freedom and promise, we find in Genesis 1 an overarching pattern of creation, profoundly influencing humanity and its relationship with God: work and rest; life and death; beginnings, endings, and new beginnings. As we read in Ecclesiastes 3:1–8, for everything there is a season.

The Adventure of Evolution

Some Christians, commonly called "creationists," read Genesis 1 as a scientific treatise, describing a literal and factual pattern of creation unfolding over the course of seven consecutive days or seven consecutive ages. Other Christians, following a figurative approach, view Genesis 1 as a literary work that uses poetic elements to arrange God's pattern of creation topically rather than sequentially or chronologically. Still other Christians accept the reality of evolution and posit God's guidance of the evolutionary process. Many traditionalist Christians, however, find it difficult to accept the notion that creation and evolution belong together. The belief that such concepts are opposing and conflicting is so ingrained in the minds of many that it is hard for them to conceptualize how the God of the Bible may work out creative purposes through an evolutionary process.

Affirming original goodness and continual creation challenges the traditional doctrine of the fall, which emphasizes human sin and divine retribution. However, as theologian Brian McLaren notes, "when one takes known sin seriously but no more seriously than one should, later elements in the biblical narrative (election, redemption, revelation, salvation, eschatology) are themselves understood and integrates as glorious unfolding of continuing creation . . . Seen this way, creation is revalued and made sacred again."[2]

The key point is that evolutionary biology, now supported and widened by cosmology, has made us realize that we live in an unfinished universe. Scientific and religious systems, together with living species and all of the cosmos, are part of a process still coming into being. The history of religion, like that of science, is a long series of partially successful but mostly inadequate human attempts to adapt to the inexhaustible depths of the cosmos (which, in part, we label "God"). Religion tries to adapt humans to the world's depth through various symbols, myths, and creeds. However, the infinite elusiveness of this depth forever evades exhaustive depiction. Hence, the religious quest, like that of science, is always

---

2. McLaren, *Generous Orthodoxy*, 265–66.

frustratingly incomplete. Thus we humans, much more than animals and plants, often feel a sharp sense of dislocation and lack of correspondence to our world because we are made to adapt, not just to actuality (to what is), but even more to possibility (to what we can be, which we call "promise"). We are, in other words, "genetically wired for a world forever open to the future."[3] The fact that the universe is even now perhaps in the early phases of its full emergence helps us understand why, religiously speaking, we remain always somewhat in the dark; why our answers to our biggest questions will always be frustratingly opaque; why we must walk by faith as well as by sight; and why it makes more sense to hope than to yield to despair. The physical universe is a work in progress, and religions, firmly embedded within nature itself, are continuous with this evolutionary responsiveness. This process of adaptation can by definition never reach a static point of completion. Hence, the enormous amount of time involved in cosmic, biological, cultural, and religious evolution should come as no surprise, theologically speaking. Theology after Darwin can now suggest that the universe, understood as an adaptive process, evolves at all only because in the remote reaches of its endless depth there beckons something like a promise (this is akin to what theologians call "providence"). Promise (providence) is not manipulation of nature, but is instead a reservoir of possibilities offered to the world throughout its creative spread.

Living in a post-Darwinian universe, where evolution is a fact of life, does not demand that we give up the idea of God. Rather it asks that we think about God in a fresh way. Evolutionary knowledge, accepted and rightly viewed, can help blunt centuries of world-fleeing mystical spirituality and align our religious existence with the natural zest for life that links us biologically to our evolutionary past. The inherent adventurousness of religion may then receive a new birth. For a growing number of Christians today, evolution is a helpful and even a necessary ingredient in our thinking about God. As the Roman Catholic theologian Hans Küng put it, evolutionary theory makes possible (1) a deeper understanding of God—not as above or outside the world but as in the midst of evolution; (2) a deeper understanding of creation—not as contrary to but as making evolution possible; and (3) a deeper understanding of humans as organically related to the entire cosmos.[4]

3. Haught, *Deeper Than Darwin*, 145.
4. Küng, *Does God Exist?*, 347.

Skeptics, of course, will immediately ask how we can reconcile our ideas about a providential God with the role that chance plays in life's evolution.[5] This is a crucial question, which creationists cannot address with finality, since it questions the reality of chance, attributing it to human ignorance of some larger divine plan. Panentheists, however, while acknowledging chance to be quite real, do not find that it contradicts the idea of God. On the contrary, if there exists a loving God who is intimately related to the world, we should expect an aspect of indeterminacy or randomness in nature. The reason is simple: love typically operates not in a coercive but in a persuasive manner. It refuses to force itself upon the beloved, but instead allows the beloved—in this case the entire created cosmos—to remain itself, though in such a way as to imply intimacy rather than abandonment.

If, as our religious traditions have always insisted, God truly cares for the wellbeing of the world, then the world must be permitted to be something other than God. Even if it derives its being fundamentally from God, it must have a certain amount of "freedom" or autonomy. If the world did not somehow exist on its own, it would be nothing more than an extension of God's own being, and hence not be a world unto itself. If the world is to be anything distinct from God, it has to have room for experimenting with different ways of existing. Leaving room for such latitude does not mean that there is no divine vigilance, but only that out of respect for the otherness of creation, divine love does not crudely intrude. God risks allowing the cosmos to exist in relative liberty, and in the story of life, the world's inherent "freedom" manifests itself through the random variations or genetic mutations that comprise the raw material of evolution. A certain amount of chance is consonant with a panentheistic understanding of God.

If God were a magician or a dictator, then we might expect the universe to be finished all at once and to remain eternally unchanged. But what an impoverished world that would be! It would lack all the drama, diversity, adventure, and intense beauty that evolution has in fact produced. A world of human design might have a listless harmony to it, and it might be a world devoid of pain and struggle, but it would have none of the novelty, contrast, danger, upheaval, and grandeur provided by evolution over billions of years.

---

5. The material in the remainder of this segment is adapted from Haught, *Science and Religion*, 61–63.

Fortunately, the God of our perspective is not a magician but a creator. And this God is more interested in promoting freedom and the adventure of evolution than in preserving the status quo. The long creative struggle of the universe to arrive at life, consciousness, and culture is consonant with the conviction that real love never forces a particular outcome but always allows for freedom, risk, adventure—and also suffering—on the part of the beloved.

Viewed in this light, the evolution of the cosmos is more than just compatible with faith in a God of self-giving love; it actually anticipates an evolving universe. It would be very difficult for us to reconcile the religious teaching about God's infinite self-giving love with any other kind of cosmos.

Questions for Discussion and Reflection

1. Since the doctrines of God and creation appear linked, both biblically and theologically, how might changes in our understanding of God impact our understanding of the doctrine of creation?

2. Does the biblical doctrine of creation focus primarily on origins (of the cosmos and of humans) or relationships (between humans and God, others, and themselves), and thereby with human meaning and purpose in the universe?

3. How would you respond to a person who argues that the accounts found in Genesis 1–11 are mythological?

4. If the notion of evolution is determined to be compatible with Christian teaching, what is it about Darwin's version of evolution that has been so disturbing? Can Darwin's theory of evolution actually enhance one's understanding of God? Explain your answer.

5. Assess the merits of the panentheist position regarding science and religion? Are you optimistic that greater numbers of traditional Christians might commit to this perspective? What problems remain to be worked out?

6. Do you find the notion of "promise" in the universe attractive? Why or why not?

Chapter 8

Rethinking Jesus and the Incarnation

WE HAVE BEEN STATING all along that the primary problem in human consciousness—one manifested in conventional religious teaching—is dualistic thinking, that is, a mindset that perceives reality as divided into metaphysical polarities or opposing entities: good versus evil, spirit versus matter, God versus Satan. Nondualist or holistic thinking does accept the existence of opposites or distinctions in nature, such as maleness and femaleness, lightness and darkness, active and passive, but they are viewed on a continuum and thus as interrelated.

This ultimate relatedness of all things in the universe is best exemplified by the striking Eastern concept called the Tao (pronounced dhow), which speaks of "the way" of reality, the orderly movement of the natural world according to the principle of yin and yang. This is best depicted by the famous Chinese symbol of a circle divided by a backward or reverse S into light and dark (or red and yellow) areas. According to Taoist teaching, yin is the negative force in nature. Understood as passive, it is seen in darkness, coolness, dampness, and femaleness, and is represented earth, specifically by the moon. Yang is the positive force in nature. Understood as active, it is seen in lightness, warmth, dryness, maleness, and is represented by heaven, specifically by the sun.

All things are on a continuum between yin and yang. For instance, all males have some yin, and all females some yang. These forces are not confined to humans, nor are they static. A rotting tree is said to be losing yang and becoming damp and therefore more yin. No value judgment is given to yin and yang, for neither is better than the other, and neither is solely good or solely evil. Except for a few objects, such as the sun and the earth, which in their totality are yin or yang, the rest of nature, and even events, are a combination. When the two forces work together in harmony, life is as it should be.

Because human brains are hardwired to think in binary or dualistic ways, religious scholar Cantwell Smith distinguished between "conflict dualism" and "complementary dualism." In ancient Mesopotamia, as evident in Zoroastrianism and Manicheism, we find the ideology of conflict dualism, where opposites such as good and evil or God and Satan are locked in constant war. Such ideas influenced Judaism, Christianity, and Islam, based on Greek and Western logic, in which opposites cannot be reconciled. Eastern logic, as exemplified in Taoism and certain forms of Hinduism and Buddhism, emphasizes complementary dualism (nondualist thinking).

The brilliant word, nonduality (*advaita* in Sanskrit), is used by many different traditions, both Eastern and Western, to distinguish from monism, a perspective that erases all diversity and difference, reducing all things to one sameness. Nondualism celebrates difference and affirms diversity. It simply refuses to see this diversity as anything other than the greater unity of a singular Reality.

When speaking of nondualism, Cantwell Smith spoke of complementary dualism, but the underlying reality is the same. In nature, things appear as opposites not to conflict with one another but rather to complement each other. In everything they see, think, and experience, nondualists find the dimension of the other. That is the meaning of the Tao, the circle divided into yin and yang.

C. S. Lewis seems to have had this in mind when he identified universal truths in concepts such as the Tao (the Way) in ancient China and *rita* (divine Law or Truth) in early Hinduism.[1] In Hinduism, *rita* is the principle of natural order which regulates and coordinates the operation of the universe and everything in it. Likewise the Chinese speak of the Tao as the essence of reality or the Way of the universe. The ancient Jews conceived of Torah as way, truth, and life. The author of the gospel of John seems to be alluding to this notion of a universal principle of natural order when he speaks of Jesus as the Logos (the divine Word) in John 1:1, 14 and also as the Way, the Truth, and the Life in 14:6.

---

1. Lewis, *Abolition of Man*, 27–29. In an appendix, "Illustrations of the Tao," Lewis examines eight examples of the Natural Law found in legal and religious texts across cultures of antiquity, 95–121.

The Trajectory of Incarnation

Christianity's true and unique storyline has always been incarnation. While most Christians today think of incarnation in singular terms, as a reference to the birth of Jesus, in its fullest meaning, this doctrine teaches Christians to view all reality—the spiritual and the natural, the immaterial and the physical—as one. These have always been one, ever since the Big Bang took place some 13.7 billion years ago.

Incarnation did not just happen when Jesus was born, although that is when we became aware of the human incarnation of God (the Christ) in Jesus. It seemingly took until two thousand years ago for humanity to be ready for what the Jewish philosopher Martin Buber (1878–1965) called an I-Thou relationship with God. However, matter and spirit had been one since "the beginning," when God first became manifested as creation.

What was personified in the body of Jesus was a manifestation of this universal truth: matter is, and has always been, this hiding place for Spirit, forever offering itself to be discovered anew. Perhaps this is what Jesus meant when he said, "I am the door" (John 10:7). This is what medieval Franciscan scholar John Duns Scotus (1266–1308) meant when he said that Christ was not Plan B; God did not plan to remain absent until Adam and Eve ate from the Tree of Knowledge, or until the coming of Jesus for our salvation. Rather, Christ was Plan A from the beginning, the first idea in the mind of God, as it were (John 1:1–4). In the beginning, God, the formless, eternal, and timeless One essentially said, "I am going to manifest who I am in what humans will call physicality, materiality, or the universe."

If this is true, it means that everything we have ever seen with our physical eyes is the mystery of incarnation. The Christian word for that is "the Christ," which comes from the Jewish word Messiah or Anointed One, a reference to the One who would come to reveal what God is doing, everywhere and all the time. For Christians, "the Christ" became manifested in Jesus of Nazareth, a view biblical scholars call "the scandal of particularity."

In this respect, Christians come to see the mystery of incarnation in one concrete moment. Therein is its strength. However, that is not the whole truth of incarnation. What most Christians miss when they fall in love with the vulnerable newborn babe at Christmas is that what is true in one particular place is true universally, meaning that what is true for the particular ends up being true everywhere.

Christians must move beyond a merely sentimental understanding of Christmas, with its particularist application of Jesus' birth and death as the sole means of salvation, to an adult and communal appreciation of the message of the incarnation of God in Christ. Redemption (salvation) is a necessary part of incarnation, already present in Jesus' birth, because in that birth God was telling humanity that it is good to be human, for God is on the side of humanity, fully like us, yet fully unlike us.

The celebration of Christmas is not merely a sentimental remembrance of the birth of a child. It is much more a celebration of the rebirth of history. According to the apostle Paul, creation is forever pregnant with new birth, always waiting for the participation of humanity with God in its renewal (Rom 8:20–23). To focus solely on the birth of a baby at Christmas is to be content with "infant Christianity."

In incarnation, God clearly wants friends and partners to image divine diversity. God, it seems, want mature religion and a thoughtful, free response from human beings. In incarnation, God beckons us to partnership, and as it happens, we eventually become the God that we love.

The Third Incarnation of God

When ordinary people become Christians, that is, "little Christ's," they embody or enact in their lives the "third incarnation" of God, or the "Second Coming" of Christ.[2] Let me explain what I mean. The first incarnation is the moment described in Genesis 1 as "the first day," when God became the Universal Christ, joining in unity with the physical universe and becoming the light inside of everything. This is described in Genesis 1:3–4 by the statement, "Then God said, 'Let there be light'; and there was light . . . and God separated the light from the darkness." This teaching is affirmed in the prologue of John's gospel, by the relationship between God and Christ (the Word/Logos): "In the beginning was the Word, and the Word was with God, and the Word was God . . . in him was life, and the life was the light of all people. The light shines in the darkness, and the darkness did not overcome it" (John 1:1, 4–5). The first incarnation—what we might call the Universal Christ—is the divine presence

---

2. The concept of three incarnations, exemplified in what Richard Rohr calls an incarnational worldview, is articulated in his book *The Universal Christ*, 12–21.

pervading creation since the beginning. What scientists call the Big Bang is the scientific name for that event, and "Christ" is its theological name. From this perspective, wherever the material and the spiritual coincide, we have the Christ.

The second incarnation of God and the "first coming" of Christ represent what Christians believe about the historical incarnation we call Jesus. Let us be clear: Christ is not Jesus' last name. The word Christ is a title, meaning Anointed One. When Christians speak of Jesus Christ, they include the entire sweep of the meaning of the Christ, which includes all the divine activity since the beginning of time (see Rom 1:20; Heb 1:3; Col 3:11). Of this activity, Jesus is the visible map, the one who brings this eternal message home personally.

The third incarnation of God (the "Second Coming of Christ") occurs whenever true discipleship occurs, when Jesus Christ is born in us. This stunning possibility should not come as a shock, for we sing its truth every Christmas. Phillips Brooks spoke of this reality in the lyrics to the carol, *O Little Town of Bethlehem*:

> O holy Child of Bethlehem, Descend to us, we pray;
> Cast out our sin and enter in, *Be born in us today.*
> We hear the Christmas angels, the great glad tidings tell;
> *O come to us, abide with us, Our Lord Emmanuel.*

While Christmas captures the mystery of incarnation—of divine love and peace on earth—consumerism has turned it into a buying frenzy, beginning earlier each year, adding Black Friday and Cyber Monday to the "shop 'til we drop" mentality, all in an attempt to alleviated the anxiety of last minute shopping. How is it that a season of joy has become a season of depression and despair? Substituting consumption for spirituality always leaves us disappointed, unfulfilled, and wanting more: societal addiction at its worst!

Further evidence for the third incarnation appears in the Eucharist: "Eat it and know who you are," Augustine said. As any nutritionist knows, we are what we eat and drink. Christians are part of the Christ mystery. No longer alienated from God, others, or the universe—at least in principle—Christians embody cosmic belonging, oneness with Christ, the name we give to everything purposeful and harmonious in the universe. Paul affirmed this truth when he declared, "It is no longer I who live, but it is Christ who lives in me" (Gal 2:20). Exhorting believers to adopt the mind of Jesus (Phil 2:5), he also confirmed that Christians incarnate

Christ, since they possess "the mind of Christ" (1 Cor 2:16). When individuals become Jesus people—incarnations of Christ—they exchange one mindset for another, their "monkey mind" (the obsessive, noisy chattering we observe during silent meditation) for the mind of Christ.

Speaking humanistically, grace rarely means getting what we want, for God is not a permissive parent, but speaking spiritually, grace means always getting what we want, for our desires become the desires of Christ. This is likely what Paul meant when he called believers God's "new creation" (2 Cor 5:17): "If anyone is in Christ, there is a new creation: everything old has passed away; see, everything has become new." For Paul, when the minds of believers are transformed into the mind of Christ, their bodies become temples, dwelling places of God's Spirit (1 Cor 3:16–17; see Rom. 12:1–2).

As we travel inward, into the interior depth of soul, we discover that each believer is a chip off the old block, a miniature word of the Word of God, a mini-incarnation of divine love. This entails allowing God's grace to heal, hold, and empower us. It means entering the unknowns of our lives, and learning to trust the darkness, for the transformative power of divine love is already there.

The Christ we await at Christmas includes our own rebirth as well as the rebirth of history and creation, what the author of the book of Revelation calls "a new heaven and a new earth" (Rev 21:1). This is the cosmic Christ Christians invoke when they say, "Come, Lord Jesus" (Rev 22:20). This understanding of incarnation makes our entire lives, and the history and life of the entire cosmos, one huge "advent." "The Christ" includes the whole sweep of creation and history joined with him, as well as each of us. This togetherness is the Universal or Cosmic Christ. To use biblical imagery, the followers of this Jesus are members of the "body of Christ," even though they are not the historical Jesus. So Christians rightly believe in "Jesus Christ," and both words are essential.

Son of Man/Son of God

Theism believes there is a God. Christianity affirms that God and humanity coexist in the same body, in the same place. These beliefs seem antithetical, for they are utterly different proclamations about the nature of the universe. The dualist mind can accept one or the other—rarely both. In this respect, Jesus is understood to be either divine or human, never

Rethinking Jesus and the Incarnation

fully both, and we think of ourselves as merely humans trying desperately to become "spiritual." Overcoming this divide is the point of the incarnation of God in Jesus.

The manifestation of the divine "I Am" in Jesus (John 8:58; 10:30) was the momentous Christian epiphany. This became so thrilling to early Christians that they overlooked the continued need to balance Jesus' divinity with an even more strongly proclaimed humanity (see Heb 4:15; Gal 4:4). In this regard, we need to recall that virtually Jesus' only form of self-reference in the synoptic gospels is *ben 'adam* (Son of Man), that is, a son of the human one (Matt 8:20; see Ps 8:4).³ In using this phrase repeatedly, Jesus was emphasizing he was one of us—mortal and human.

C. S. Lewis, a former atheist who converted to evangelical Christianity and gained fame as an apologist for traditional Christianity in the mid-twentieth century, famously argued that three options—and three alone—are available for people in thinking about Jesus Christ: either he was a liar, a self-deceived lunatic, or else he was what Christians have traditionally affirmed, Son of God, Lord of all, and therefore God in human flesh. Despite my appreciation for Lewis and his distinctive writings, I find these options inadequately narrow and woefully misguided, for Jesus does not literally fit any of these categories. They emerge from the perspective of the Precritical Paradigm, from reading the gospels as if they were straightforward historical documents.

Such a reading distorts the image of Jesus, for it focuses exclusively on his deity, emphasizing the miraculous—especially the virgin birth and the physical bodily resurrection. Concentrating on the saving significance of Jesus' death (that he died for our sins), this approach concludes that Jesus and Christianity are the only way of salvation. Furthermore, it places head knowledge—belief—at the center of Christianity, stressing that to be a Christian requires affirmation that all of the above are factually true.

Modern scholarship discounts such narrow understanding of Jesus and views literalistic interpretations of scripture as misleading. In our attempts to rethink our understanding of Jesus, it is vital that we start with the humanity of Jesus (what scholars call "Christology from below")⁴ rather that with his preexistence and deity (what scholars call "Christology

---

3. However much the Son of Man expression was developed later by the church, Jesus' use of the term is a paradoxical way to refer to himself as a lowly mortal.

4. The term Christology refers to the Christian doctrine of the person and significance of Christ.

from above"). It is possible to move from the humanity of Jesus to his divinity, but not from his divinity to his humanity. That was the path available to the first believers, and the only path available to us. The key is to begin where the first Christians began, with their relationship with Jesus of Nazareth, the teacher and role model they knew, trusted, and loved, and then to press forward with the development of that understanding in understanding the church's experience of Christ. If we start with Jesus, we understand better who we are as humans and what we can become. If we start with Christ, we stand to lose our present and our future, our human actuality as well as our human potentiality.

As Martin Luther noted: The "humanity [of Jesus] is our holy ladder, by which we ascend to the knowledge of God. . . . Who wishes safely to ascend to the love and knowledge of God . . . let him first exercise himself in the humanity of Christ."[5] For Luther, "The scriptures begin very gently, and lead us on to Christ as a man, and then to one who is Lord over all creatures, and after that to one who is God. So do I enter delightfully, and learn to know God. But the [church] philosophers and doctors have insisted on beginning from above, and so they have become fools. We must begin from below, and after that come upwards."[6]

There are, as Luther indicates, two types of Christology, "from below" and "from above." Both types can be expressed in orthodox or in heterodox ways, and both are present in the New Testament. The earliest heretical movements in Christianity, however, tended to overspiritualize Jesus, dissociating the spiritual Christ from the physical Jesus and thereby attempting to detach Christianity from history. Such views, gnostic in nature, found agreement in docetic views of Christ, denying he was ever a true human being. A basic conviction of the Greco-Roman world was that truth, eternal and supernatural, was changeless, and that it could not (or should not) be tied to ephemeral phenomena or transitory events. By inserting the name "Pontius Pilate," the Roman procurator who authorized the crucifixion of Jesus, into the second article of the Apostles' Creed, orthodox Christians were emphasizing the historicity of the Christian faith as grounded in a series of historical events while counteracting dualistic views of reality.

---

5. Luther, *Weimarer Ausgabe* 57.99.3; cited in Hamilton, *New Essence of Christianity*, 88.

6. Luther, *Weimarer Ausgabe* 10/I 2.297.5; English translation taken from Mackintosh, *Person of Jesus Christ*, 232.

Rethinking Jesus and the Incarnation

Traditional Christianity has had a large stake in historicity. From the start, much of classical Christology—particularly the doctrine of the two natures—has depended on being able to regard the words and deeds of Jesus in the gospels as actual and reliable, and the resurrection, equated with the empty tomb as historical fact, has been seen as the hinge of the Christian faith. Yet modern Christians cannot escape the evaluation of critical biblical scholarship, which asserts that there is no certainty that Jesus did or said most of the things attributed to him in scripture.

The skepticism of the postmodern ethos, which questions traditional language about the mystery of Christ, has shattered the beliefs of the past, reducing universal religious, metaphysical, and moral truths to tentative, private, and subjective claims and opinions. The classic way of expressing ultimate reality had been to use the vocabulary of uniqueness, of finality, of timeless perfection. That Christian theology presented Jesus Christ as *the* Son of God and *the* Son of Man, *the* Alpha and *the* Omega, in whom all lines meet uniquely, perfectly, and finally. Our world, however, relativistic, pluralistic, and diverse, compels us to be more modest about our claims. For many today, to go on saying the same things in the old terms is to be in danger of rendering Christ meaningless, the answer to questions few are asking.

Thankfully, as we are discovering, the static model of reality is largely unbiblical, the imposition of a later and alien culture. The Bible is much more at home with God as active and dynamic, who confronts humans in and through the particularities and peculiarities of the here and now. The Bible does not portray God as one who is unmoved by human need, who lags behind social and biological change, but as one who is characteristically found on the shifting frontiers of such change and need, incarnated in mundane and timely events rather than in a timeless absolute beyond them all.

With regard to the historical Jesus, two closely connected questions arise: "What *can* we know of him?" and "What do we *need* to know?" The latter question, of course, is significantly more important. Our intent is not to reduce God or Christ to our level, but to relocate "the beyond" and "the ancient," the absolute and the metaphysical, to our midst. This does not mean denying the dimension of transcendence or the supernatural, but it does mean starting where modern skeptics and postmodern seekers might have the best chance of encounter. It means beginning with the familiar and the contingent. In this process, the claims of honesty and integrity, of justice and freedom, of solidarity with universal suffering may be taken seriously and without reserve. One may not see how it all adds up or discern any final truths or laws that cannot be broken, but in the particular, concrete situation, one knows that persons matter more than procedures, principles more than precepts.

Today, in our cultural milieu, the place of theology in general and of Christology and soteriology in particular, is the servants' quarters, not, as in the period of Christendom, the throne. Its style will be more modest, more broken. Yet at its center is a figure, as the author of Hebrews insists he always is, who is "suited to our need" (Heb 7:26, NEB), and whom in all his humiliation Christians still rightly call "Teacher" and "Master" (John 13:13).

Whatever more he is—or was—he must be one of us. If Jesus is to be our Person, our Man, he must be a human being in every sense of the word. This is what we find in the New Testament. The early Christians began with a view of Christ that was uncomplicated and relatable. They certainly did not see Jesus to be of *merely* human significance, since he embodied what God was doing in their midst. But their earliest memory was fashioned into a simplistic Christology, perhaps the earliest, of "a man," Jesus of Nazareth, singled out by God, crucified and raised from the dead, as Peter's speech on the day of Pentecost recalls (Acts 2:22–24). "This Jesus God raised up, and of that all of us are witnesses. Being therefore exalted at the right hand of God, and having received from the Father the promise of the Holy Spirit, he has poured out this that you both see and hear" (Acts 2:32–33).

John Knox has made the point that as long as this primitive "adoptionist" or "exaltationist" Christology prevailed, "the simple actuality of the humanity was in no sense or degree compromised. Not only could it be whole and intact, but it was also subject to no theological or mythological pressure of any kind."[7] But the pressure began soon thereafter, when the idea that the death of Jesus was according to "the definite plan and foreknowledge of God" (Acts 2:23) became translated as the preexistence of Christ. As soon as Jesus Christ was, or could be, represented as a preexistent being who had come down from heaven, then the genuineness of his humanity while he was on earth was open to question. Not that his followers actually questioned his humanity, for the memory was too strong. From the beginning of theological reflection on the significance of Jesus there was the insistence on his solidarity with humanity; otherwise

---

7. Knox, *Humanity and Divinity of Christ*, 6–7.

his relevance for us would be undercut. Nevertheless, the threat to his humanity was there, precisely because of the story told about him to bring out the significance of his humanity for our salvation.

The Christian affirmation is that Jesus is both human and divine, simultaneously, something that applies both to Jesus and by extension, to ourselves (see John 1:12; 14:12). As the Christian scriptures affirm, we humans are already spiritual (we are "in Christ" and therefore in God), and our difficult but necessary task is to learn how to be human. Jesus models the full integration for us (1 Cor 15:47–49). He told us, in effect, that divinity looked just like him—while he appeared ordinarily human to his contemporaries.

It is the nondual mind that allows us to affirm the infinite mystery of Jesus and the infinite mystery of our own being. These are finally the same mystery.

God and Gender

Humans tend to imitate the God they worship. For that reason alone, our conception of God is vital to human wellbeing. To view God abstractly, as sexless or inanimate, might work for certain mystics, but for most of us, God is personal. However, for too long, God has been gendered as masculine, and that has led to hierarchical and patriarchal patterns upholding competitive, authoritarian, oppositional, impositional, and even violent values—individually, corporately, institutionally, and nationally.

Unfortunately, this imbalance on the yang dimension of life can force the Daoist pendulum to shift to the other side of the spectrum, where masculine features are devalued in favor of feminine qualities. Societies, communities, and organizations based on feminist overreaction, while occasionally needed to balance the scale, can also create imbalance and disharmony. Because our society still tilts toward the yang side, favoring male privilege, we focus here on the need for balanced views of God.

While it is common theoretically to think of God as sexless, to conceptualize God as personal leads naturally to envision God as either male, female, or some combination of both. When our earliest human ancestors worshipped or conceptualized deity, they thought holistically, envisioning God in unified ways, as the totality of ultimate Reality. Later polytheists, thinking more specifically, envisioned many powers and gods, arranged in hierarchical order. In this way of thinking, the gods were conceptualized as male and female, cohabiting with one another and even on occasion with humans. Eventually, particularly with the emergence of institutionalized Western religions such as Judaism, Christianity, and Islam, God was gendered as masculine and, by virtue of his role as Creator, the apex of power, life, and morality.

Vestiges of these stages are found embedded in the Hebrew scriptures. For example, when early Jews and Christians read the accounts of creation in Genesis, they read them literally, consecutively, and chronologically. Thus, when God created the first human in Genesis 1:26–27, they understood this man ('adam) to be made in the divine image and likeness, uniting in that primal being maleness and femaleness. Reading literally and consecutively, they found in Genesis, not two different accounts of the creation of human beings, but two consecutive accounts of their creation. When read in this manner, Adam (humanity) was created twice. In chapter 1, God made human beings according to God's image: "male and female he created them" (1:27). In the original Hebrew text, it is not clear whether God made multiple human beings who were either male or female, or whether God made a single androgynous human being. In chapter 2, creation seems to start over again, and that is probably how most ancient people read these stories—as one continuous account. Hence, God made the male Adam and placed him in a garden, for God could find no suitable partner for Adam from among the animals. Thus, God constructed a female mate for Adam from Adam's rib. If in Genesis 1 God created an androgynous human being, who was both male and female, then in chapter 2 God separated the human being into male and female. God did so by removing the female (the rib) from the male. This process does not emphasize equality, however, for the female appears to be less than the male. This explains why most ancient people did not think of male and female as equal partners, for the Genesis account presents the female as a derivative aspect of the male, and therefore as not fully male. Predictably, this inequality continues to this day among traditionalist Christians.

Later reading of scripture by Jews and Christians living in male dominated hierarchical societies retained not only monarchical images but also masculine images of God, a pattern that has predominated in Western society to our time, despite the efforts of biblical scholars, who find feminine images and representations of the divine throughout scripture.

When Christians speak of incarnation, they tend to think first of Jesus, and then perhaps of the rest of creation. When thinking of the incarnation, it is easy to focus on masculinity, for all the personages involved seem to be male. But that view, limited and dangerous, is also defective and incomplete. For no incarnation can take place without a real feminine presence and polarity. While traditionalist Christians tend to think of the Virgin Mary in this respect, this is not what I have in mind, for at best, that version of incarnation is partial and misconstrued.

For too long now, Christians have forgotten the feminine aspect of God, which is why we are witnessing an immense longing for relational, mutually empowering feminine qualities at every level of our society. Left primarily in the hands of men for most of history, our politics, economics, psyches, culture, patterns of leadership, and our theologies have all become far too competitive, argumentative, and individualistic. The feminine aspect of God was much valued by Christians of the first three centuries of the common era, including those associated with Valentinian and gnostic forms of Christianity as well as by theologians such as Origen of Alexandria (c. 185–c. 254), whose theology, though controversial, set the agenda for Christian thought for centuries to come. A return to the Hebrew version of the Genesis account of creation brings us in touch with the feminine, co-creative Spirit (*ruach*) of God (see Gen 1:2), also called Wisdom (*hochmah*) in Hebrew and Sophia in Greek.

At the center of Israel's wisdom literature stands Sophia, a biblical personification of wisdom. In the book of Proverbs particularly, the extent and significance of the personifications are so great that wisdom appears as more than a literary character. In Proverbs 1–9 and implicitly elsewhere in the book, we find reference to wisdom as a figure who speaks frequently in the first person and identifies herself not just as the divine companion, but also as the source of order in society and success in life (8:15–21). In Proverbs 8:22–30, wisdom speaks of herself as having been created before anything else and as God's companion and even assistant at the creation of the cosmos.

Several things should be said about this intriguing poem. First, its bold use of feminine imagery. Wisdom is not explicitly called God's daughter, but the poem verges on that meaning. Second, wisdom is portrayed as being with God at the beginning, but not as co-eternal with God, or as a "goddess." She is subordinate to God, "the first" of God's acts, preexisting all else in creation. Third, the language is metaphorical, as is all God-language, for God is beyond all gender categories, including distinctions of masculinity or femininity. Significantly, this poem breaks out of the masculine metaphors that dominate much of scripture, continually making use of feminine imagery.

Who is Lady Wisdom, this alluring figure of poetry? Is she merely a literary fiction? Is she a personification of the order and harmony in the universe? Is she a personification of Torah, or of an attribute of God? In the Hellenistic period, Jews began to think of wisdom as the Word of God (Sir 24:3), and therefore, like Torah (Sir 15:1; 19:20; 24:23), indistinguishable from God's mind, will, and love. She is the thread that ties together all of reality. In the Wisdom of Solomon, the last of the Jewish wisdom books, her identification with God is made more explicit. She is described as "the fashioner of all things" (7:22) and equated with God's Spirit (7:22–27; 9:17). In the Bible, to live wisely, to embrace wisdom and to live with her is, finally, to live with God. Such living recognizes, collaborates, and is transformed by the harmony, beauty, and order of God in this world.

It is not a big leap from here to the Christian understanding of the Holy Spirit or to christological passages in the New Testament, such as the connection of the divine Logos to Jesus (John 1:1), the Word of God, or to Jesus, the "firstborn of all creation" (Col 1:15). The personification of wisdom in Proverbs introduces a type of speculation that we encounter in later Christian theological discussion of the three persons of the Trinity.

As Christopher Pramuk writes, "Sophia is the *eros* of God become one with all creation, the love in God that longs for incarnation from before the beginning. She is the co-creativity of God, always inviting, never compelling, coming to birth in us when we say yes to [what Thomas Merton called] 'the dawning of divine light in the stillness of our hearts.'"[8]

Mystics of the world's religions, including the Western traditions of Judaism, Christianity, and Islam, affirm the profoundly feminine understanding of God found in panentheism, the theological and cosmological perspective that views all particles of the universe to be infused with the progressive and creative nature of God, said to interpenetrate the universe while remaining greater than all that is. According to the panentheistic perspective, human beings live in a Christ-soaked world, a world where matter is inspirited and spirit is embodied. In such a world, everything is sacred.

---

8. Pramuk, *At Play in Creation*, 5–6.

Questions for Discussion and Reflection

1. Before reading this chapter, what was your understanding of the doctrine of incarnation? After reading this chapter, has your understanding changed? Why or why not?

2. This chapter begins with an explanation of the Eastern concept called the Tao. What does the principle of yin and yang contribute to your understanding of the Christian doctrine of incarnation?

3. In your estimation, what did the medieval theologian John Duns Scotus mean when he said that Christ was not God's Plan B?

4. After reading this chapter, explain the differences and similarities between the terms "Christ" and "Jesus." Which one came first chronologically? Explain the importance of this distinction.

5. Explain and assess the merits of the "third incarnation of God."

6. Evaluate the merits of C. S. Lewis's three options for thinking about Jesus Christ. Explain why the author of this book finds these options inadequate.

7. Explain the difference between "Christology from below" and "Christology from above." Before reading this chapter, which of these perspectives best represented your view? After reading this chapter, have your views changed? Why or why not?

8. Explain the problems that emerge historically and socially when we attribute gender to God. In your estimation, how does the Bible conceptualize God, as male, female, as both, or as neither? Explain your answer. In your estimation, does our answer matter? Why or why not?

Chapter 9

The Historical Jesus and Apocalyptic Theology, Part I[1]

IN THIS CHAPTER, I return to the topic of my first biblical commentary, a study on the book of Revelation.[2] There, I explored how Revelation and its apocalyptic message might be read and interpreted sensibly in the twenty-first century. Here I return to this topic to unpack more clearly and realistically what the book of Revelation meant to the original audience, to early Christians marginalized by threat, ridicule, and persecution. For them, belief brought hope of survival, for they were convinced that God was about to invade history decisively, overthrowing Roman oppression and instituting a millennial kingdom of peace and righteousness on earth.

As we saw in chapter 4, the role of religion is to contribute a third dimension to life, adding spirituality to rationality and physicality. However, for the past two millennia, the religious impetus originating in the Middle East has been hijacked by an alien element, a cancer that infiltrated not only the monotheistic religions of Judaism, Christianity, and Islam but also human consciousness as a whole with a feeling of pessimism regarding the human condition and even nature as a whole. This feeling became a belief, and then a central dogma of Christianity, resulting in the conviction that, if left to its own devices and resources, humanity and nature were doomed. Those who hold this belief are succumbing to the ideology of apocalypticism, the mindset that fueled the birth and growth of early Christianity.

1. Chapters 9 and 10 form one continuous narrative.
2. Vande Kappelle, *Hope Revealed*.

End-Time Theology: A Historical Overview

In the fall of 2020, during the COVID-19 epidemic, I unexpectedly met Rabbi Dave, a ministerial colleague from my time as a college chaplain and professor. Having retired as an academic, I was back in Washington, Pennsylvania on a routine doctor's visit when I stopped at a local mall to pick up some supplies. Despite wearing masks, Dave and I recognized each other instantly. Earlier, as a professor of religious studies, I had visited the local synagogue various times, and for a time, Rabbi Dave taught courses in my department. I had asked him to read some of my manuscripts, which he gladly endorsed.

After a few words of greeting, I was surprised to hear my old friend state, almost matter-of-factly, that he believed we were living in "the last days." This phrase, clearly an apocalyptic notion, reflects the belief, common to first-century Jews and Christians, that they were living at a dire time, in expectation of divine intervention, when normal life on earth would end and a new, utopian age would be inaugurated by divine action.

Significantly, apocalyptic Christianity was the form of religion in which I had been raised and indoctrinated, a biblical form of Christianity based primarily upon a literal reading of the Bible. As a child reared in Costa Rica by missionary parents, my youthful worldview had been framed by two all-encompassing realities: sin and salvation. The cause of all problems on earth, human and natural, I learned, is sin—understood as the consequence of human autonomy and rebellion against divine authority—and the solution is salvation—understood as repentance from sin, which results in spiritual rebirth and in the promise of eternal life with God in heaven. Those of us alive now are living in "the last days" of human history, in expectation of the return of Christ to earth to rescue his followers from the Great Tribulation that is to come, instituted by a figure known as the Antichrist, who will arise in the aftermath of the church's rapture to heaven at Christ's return. My parents were "premillennial dispensationalists," and I was assured that this perspective, popular among evangelical Christians, was taught by scripture. According to the sin/salvation paradigm, the Christian life is about correct theology and proper ethics. However, underlying all true religion is a special insight: The world as we know it is about to end, and those who are "born again" will soon be taken from this evil world, "raptured" to a good and perfect divine realm known as heaven, where true believers will live eternally with God and with one another. Only a remnant of Christians, and only this group, will experience eternal life. The rest of humanity, including past and future generations, will be lost eternally and consigned to divine torment. As a true believer, I had assurance of my salvation, and that meant that I was responsible to share life's special truth with others, always prepared to offer a reasonable explanation to those who inquire about "the hope that is in us" (see 1 Pet 3:15), a hope of the Second Coming of Christ (see Titus 2:13).

This dualistic perspective, based on eschatological and apocalyptic views found in the Bible, underlay the belief system of many early Christians. It has continued in all ages and forms of Christianity since its inception, emerging passionately and convincingly in times of crisis, uncertainty, and rapid change. At such times, however, opposing Christian voices arose, equally passionately and convincingly—denouncing such views as ignorant and deluded.[3]

There has never been a time in the church's history when there hasn't been some prophecy concerning the time and manner of Christ's return. Ends and beginning play a large part in humanity's experience of itself, not least in the Judeo-Christian tradition. Apocalypses—the revelation or unveiling of the world's destiny and of humanity's—have fascinated Jews and Christians for the last two millennia. In his 1999 book, *Apocalypses*, Eugen Weber narrates humankind's unshakeable belief that the end of time is at hand, unraveling the mysteries and patterns of millennial thought. While I recommend that work for its breadth and empathy, for our purposes, I follow the summary given by Bart Ehrman in *Jesus: Apocalyptic Prophet of the New Millennium*, also written in 1999.

In his work, Ehrman provides six examples of end-time scenarios, working back from the present to the teachings of Jesus, who, like many of his followers, taught that the world would come to a sudden halt in the near future, during his lifetime or certainly in his generation. Through this event, the fulfillment of the "Day of the Lord" predicted long before by Hebrew prophets, God would intervene in the affairs of this planet, overthrowing the forces of evil in a cosmic act of judgment. As a result, God's coming would establish a utopian kingdom here on earth.

Ehrman's account begins in 1988, with the publication of Edgar Whisenant's *88 Reasons Why the Rapture Will Be in 1988*. Whisenant, a former NASA rocket engineer, used a literalist approach to biblical prophecies that led him to his conclusion. Of course, he was wrong, for

---

3. Weber, *Apocalypses*, 3–5.

the end never did come. In 1970, Hal Lindsey published his *The Late Great Planet Earth*, predicting that a thermonuclear holocaust would engulf the planet by the late 1980s. His book, packed with anecdotes and plausible historical scenarios, read like a detective novel, becoming the best-selling work of nonfiction (in retrospect, the category should have been "fiction) of the 1970s.

Perhaps the best-known date-setter of American history is William Miller, an uneducated farmer whose literalistic reading of Daniel 8:14 led to "The Great Disappointment" of October 22, 1844, when thousands of followers gave away all their possessions in the belief that Jesus would soon appear. Moving the clock backward to the tenth century, we come across Joachim of Fiore, an official in Silicia (now southern Italy) who had a series of visions in which he claimed to have learned directly from God the mysteries that would unlock the meaning of the Bible and the course of human history. In 1171 he entered a Benedictine monastery, and over a period of eighteen years he wrote and discussed his prophecies. Refusing to name the specific time of the end, he strongly suggested that it would happen in the next century. A couple of decades after his death, some Franciscan monks, building on his writings, claimed that the world as they knew it was going to come to an end in the year 1260. As you might have guessed, it didn't.

Moving backward to the second century, we continue to find prominent Christian groups proclaiming the imminent end of history, including the followers of a self-proclaimed prophet named Montanus. One of the reasons the Montanists have been seen as important historically is that Tertullian, one of the most prominent theologians in the history of the church, joined their ranks at the height of his career. The Montanists held strict ethical standards for themselves and their followers, believing that the end was near and that people needed to prepare for it. In particular, Montanus believed that the new Jerusalem was to descend from heaven to his small town of Pepuza, an insignificant place in the province of Phrygia, in what is now west-central Turkey. That is where the kingdom of God would arrive and Christ would then reign. Christians should devote themselves to its coming, standing up for their faith to the point of being martyred, if necessary.

It appears that just about every generation since the beginning of Christianity until today has had its apocalyptic visionaries. This was certainly true of Jesus' early followers. In this respect, no one is more prominent than the apostle Paul, who indicates in his earliest known letter, the first letter to the Thessalonians (written fewer than twenty years after the death of Jesus), that he expects members of his audience, including himself, to be alive at the return of Christ to earth (1 Thess 4:15–17). Moving still further backward in time, we come finally to Jesus, who seems to have inspired this entire Christian tradition. Sometime around the year 30 CE he went to Jerusalem during a Passover feast, and was arrested, tried, and crucified. What views of the end time did he have, and why was he crucified?

Some clues are provided in Mark's gospel, the earliest gospel in the New Testament, considered the most reliable of the gospels because it was written within a generation of the death of Jesus (no later than 70 CE). In that gospel Jesus tells his disciples, "Truly I tell you, some of you standing here will not taste death before they have seen the kingdom of God has come with power" (9:1). Later, in the so-called Markan apocalypse, Jesus states, "Truly I tell you, this generation will not pass away until all these things have taken place" (13:30). At his trial before the Jewish high priest, Jesus is also quoted as saying, "You will see the Son of Man . . . coming with the clouds of heaven" (14:62). Is it possible that the historical Jesus, like so many of his followers in subsequent generations, predicted that the end of history as we know it would come in his own generation, or should we take all these sayings metaphorically?

From Prophecy to Apocalyptic

During the Intertestamental Period, when the culture and religion of the Jews were seriously threatened by the rise of Hellenism, a new phase of prophetic activity, known as apocalypticism, emerged. Some of its literary and theological characteristics are already perceptible in Ezekiel, Isaiah 56–66, and Zechariah 1–8. Joel 1–3 and Zechariah 9–14, in addition to Isaiah 24–27, are later examples of this category. However, the classic representation of this type of literature in the Old Testament canon is Daniel, written during the Maccabean crisis of 168–165 BCE.

While the distant future was not central to the prophets, it was not overlooked, for eschatology was basic to the prophetic message. Israel's prophets consistently looked beyond the present, in which God's purpose seemed to be temporarily opposed by Israel's rebellion, to a time when God would triumph over the forces of evil. Prophetic predictions of the triumph of God's purpose were expressed in phrases like "the Day of the

Lord," "the Age to Come," and "the Kingdom of God." In their vision the consummation of history was to be a time of reckoning, when all rebellious powers would be judged and destroyed. It was also to be the beginning of a New Creation in which nature and human nature would be transformed. No longer would there be war, and even wild animals would be tame (Isa 65:17–25). The pictures of the messianic age remind us of the idyllic peace and harmony of the Garden of Eden prior to the expulsion. The prophets proclaimed that the Day was imminent, as near as the next moment of history.

The theme of apocalyptic literature, which flourished in the postexilic period, was, like that of prophecy, the nearness of the time when God would assert sovereignty over history and nature. It is characteristic of apocalyptic, however, that specific historical events receded into the background, and the contest between God and rebellious forces assumed a cosmic scale. Apocalyptic writers were dualistic in their view of history. They perceived two dominions (kingdoms) struggling for dominance. The kingdom of God stands opposed to the well-organized kingdom of Evil that is under the leadership of Satan. This is not a metaphysical dualism, however, rooted in ultimate reality or in the depths of divinity, for God's original creation was good. Rather, this is a postcreation dualism rooted in creaturely rebellion against God—rebellion that is evident not only in human sin but also in cosmic revolt by celestial beings. The conflict between the forces of God and the forces of evil was eventually expressed in terms of the myth of Satan, a heavenly being who revolted against God and set up a rival kingdom into which human beings are enticed. These two dominions may also be described as two "ages" or "worlds," that is, times of history. The present "age," in the apocalyptic view, is under the dominion of evil, and it will be succeeded by the "new age," when evil is overcome and all things are made new.

The End will be heralded by unusual "signs" and cataclysms in nature. On the Day of Judgment, God (or God's messianic agent) will destroy all powers of evil and will create a new heaven and a new earth. As we see in the book of Daniel, the purpose of apocalyptic writers was to encourage the faithful to remain steadfast in a perilous hour when allegiance to God was temporarily eclipsed by foreign tyranny or the victory of evil. The use of fantastic imagery in books like Ezekiel and Daniel clearly indicates that the language was intended to be imaginative. The heart of the apocalyptic message was the certainty that God's purpose could not be frustrated—a certainty that found expression in the nearness of the End. This is the only way that a new age of peace and justice can come: God must destroy the whole evil system.

Jesus and Jewish Eschatology

As a first-century Palestinian Jew, Jesus belonged to a world where religion (theology) and politics went hand in hand. The theology was Jewish monotheism, a doctrine forged through centuries of subjugation and persecution, going back to the Babylonian exile (sixth century BCE). First-century Jews held their monotheism passionately. Theirs was not an abstract theory about the existence of one God. They believed that their God, Yahweh, was the only God, and that all others were idols. A corollary of monotheism was "election," the belief that the Jews had been chosen by this one God, making what happened to Israel of universal significance. Many Jews of Jesus' day believed that God was about to vindicate them, understanding this act as having global implications, as the means of divine judgment and/or mercy upon the rest of the world.

Ancient Jewish monotheists, believing in one God and in their status as God's elect people, while currently suffering oppression, also believed the present state of affairs to be temporary. Monotheism and election thus gave birth to eschatology, a perspective that views history as purposeful and therefore as moving toward a climactic resolution or restoration, at which time everything would be made right. First-century Jewish eschatology claimed that Yahweh would soon act within history to vindicate his people and to establish permanent justice and peace. This belief included the great promises of forgiveness articulated by biblical prophets such as Isaiah, Jeremiah, and Ezekiel. The exilic and post-exilic prophets spoke of a restoration still to be described, a liberation they described as a new exodus (see Isa 51:9–11; see also 43:2; 44:27).

In keeping with this understanding, it follows that Jesus of Nazareth might have viewed his mission as prophetic, announcing, like John the Baptist before him, God's coming kingdom. But Jesus, it seems, went beyond John's verbal role, embodying in his person and his ministry the presence of that kingdom. For Jesus, the all-encompassing rule of God was near, which when it came in its fullness, would restore Israel's role as "light to the nations" and challenge evil in all its manifestations, political, social, and economic. The coming kingdom of God was not a new sort of religion, a new moral code, or a new soteriology (a doctrine about how one might go to heaven after death). Nor was it a new sociological analysis, critique, or agenda. It was about Israel's story reaching its climax, about Israel's history moving toward its decisive moment.[4]

E. P. Sanders, in his classic text *Jesus and Judaism*, maintains that before the outbreak of the War of the Jews against Rome in 66 CE, "common Judaism" held the following hopes for the future: the restoration of the tribes of Israel; the conversion, destruction, or subjugation of the Gentiles; the renewal of Jerusalem, including a new or rebuilt temple; and the purification of God's people and their worship."[5] Whatever one makes of his idea of a common Judaism, surely the beliefs Sanders highlights were widespread among Jesus' contemporaries, as was apocalyptic eschatology in general. According to Sanders, Jesus was an apocalyptic prophet standing in the tradition of Jewish restoration theology. He shared the beliefs common in Judaism, together with this prevailing understanding of Israel's story and hope. Having established the essential Jewishness of Jesus on this topic, Sanders finds primitive Christianity to be a movement in continuity with Jesus' hopes and expectations: "The most certain fact of all is that early Christianity was an eschatological movement."[6]

New Testament scholar Dale Allison agrees, arguing persuasively that Jesus placed himself as the central figure in the eschatological end-time drama. For Allison, the historical Jesus was not a poet speaking metaphorically about judgment; rather he lived and thought apocalyptically. Citing profusely from the gospels, Allison concludes that Jesus envisaged, as did many other Jews in his time and place, "the advent, after suffering and persecution, of a great judgment, and after that a supernatural utopia, the kingdom of God, inhabited by the dead come back to life, to enjoy a world forever rid of evil and wholly ruled by God. Further, he thought that the night was far gone, the day at hand."[7] The belief of early Christians in the imminence of the end, according to Allison, originated not from the church's post-Easter expectations, but with Jesus himself.

Marcus Borg represents a growing number of modern scholars who challenge this understanding of Jesus, envisioning instead a non-eschatological Jesus, whose role, if interpreted prophetically, should be limited to that of a social prophet engaged in radical social criticism. According to

4. Borg and Wright, *Meaning of Jesus*, 31–35.
5. Sanders, *Jesus and Judaism*, 279–303.
6. Sanders, "Jesus: His Religious Type," 6.
7. Allison, *The Historical Christ*, 95.

this model, Jesus was a counter-cultural revolutionary who opposed the domination systems of his day both in person and through an alternative community of disciples, chosen to represent the New Israel of God. In Borg's view the kingdom of God represents a this-worldly social vision—a vision that empowers Christians and defines the church's ongoing role in society—rather than an other-worldly eschatological vision imposed from above and occasioned by a church raptured from this earth, an interpretation popular in many American fundamentalist and evangelical circles today.

Since it is not pedagogically acceptable to commingle eschatological and noneschatological perspectives of Jesus, scholars feel forced to take sides. Either Jesus' mindset was eschatological or it was not, and for that reason modern scholarship does not allow fence-sitting on the matter. There is no question in my mind that Jesus was clearly driven by current Jewish eschatological expectations and that he organized his ministry around those conceptions. As an eschatological prophet, however, he brought the entire package of prophecy to bear on his task, meaning that through his work and ministry he believed he was inaugurating and embodying the works of God's kingdom.

The Gospels and the Historical Jesus: Three Criteria

Biblical scholars famously distinguish between the "Jesus of history" and the "Christ of faith." While the New Testament writers had a great deal to say about the latter, what about the former? Who was Jesus of Nazareth? What did he teach, and what did he believe? The only way to know what Jesus actually taught is through the sources that survive from antiquity, namely, the four gospels. However, these books must be examined critically. To reconstruct the historical Jesus, it is not enough simply to quote verses from the Bible; every verse of the gospels must be examined carefully, not just to see what it says and to determine what it means, but more importantly, to establish whether it actually goes back to Jesus.

To establish reliability, biblical scholars have devised three major criteria for examining the gospels as historical sources for the life and teachings of Jesus. The first criterion used is called *independent attestation*. This criterion maintains that traditions that are attested independently by more than one source are more likely to be reliable than those found in only one source. The logic behind this criterion is that if two sources independently attest to a saying or deed of Jesus, then neither of them could have made it up. It is important to stress that the sources must be independent. The evidence they present is stronger than having only one witness. A saying found in both Matthew and Luke, however, is not independently attested, because both Matthew and Luke could have gotten it from Q (such as the Lord's Prayer or the Beatitudes).[8] However, a saying found in both Mark and John, or in Luke and the noncanonical gospel of Thomas, would be independently attested, because John did not use Mark, and Thomas did not use Luke. It is important to emphasize that independently attested traditions are not automatically authentic, only that they are more likely to be authentic.

Examples of this criterion include stories of Jesus associating with John the Baptist, which are found in Mark, Q, and John. Also included under this criterion are parables of Jesus in which he likens the kingdom of God to seeds sowed by a sower, attested in Mark, Q, and the gospel of Thomas. Of course, this criterion cannot disprove a single reference or one that is not multiply attested, but can only be used to indicate which traditions are more likely to be historically accurate. Simply because the Lord's Prayer comes only from Q does not mean Jesus did not actually teach it to his disciples. Similarly, just because the parable of the Good Samaritan appears only in Luke does not mean that Jesus could not have said it.

The second criterion is called *dissimilarity*. This criterion suggests that traditions that appear to work against the vested interests of the Christians who were telling them are more likely to be historically accurate than those that Christians may have invented to suit their own purposes. The logic behind this criterion is that we know that Christians were altering, and sometimes even creating, stories about Jesus. They did so to make their own points about him. Thus, if a story does not advance the vested interests of the Christians telling it, then it is not a story they would have made up. Such stories, then, survive in the tradition precisely because they really happened.

Examples of this criterion include the tradition that Jesus came from Nazareth, since Nazareth was an insignificant place, or Galilee, which had no connection with the coming Messiah (see John 1:46; also

---

8. The Q source (from the German word *Quelle*, meaning "source") is a saying source said to underlie Matthew and Luke. While the existence of Q is hypothetical and disputed, since no copies have survived, scholars disagree on whether this source was originally written or merely oral.

7:41). If Christians were to "make up" a place for Jesus to be born, it would probably be Bethlehem (the home of King David), or Jerusalem (the city of God). Other examples of this criterion include the tradition of Jesus as a carpenter (an occupation of low social status at the time), or that he was baptized by John (since this might suggest that he was a disciple and therefore spiritually inferior to John). Jesus' followers would not have created such accounts, or the story that he was betrayed by one of his own followers, or that he died by crucifixion, since no Jew expected the Messiah to be crucified as a criminal.

Like the criterion of independent attestation, this criterion can only be used to argue in favor of a tradition, not against it. It is problematic when it is used to argue that something didn't happen, such as when Jesus predicted that he would die in Jerusalem, since this is something he might have anticipated. However, Jesus' prediction that he would rise in three days does not meet this criterion, since that was exactly what his later followers said had happened. The best-case scenario, of course, is when a traditions passes both criteria. For a tradition to be credible, however, it also needs to pass a third criterion.

The final criterion is *contextual credibility*. It argues that no tradition about Jesus can be accepted as reliable if it cannot plausibly be situated in a first-century Jewish Palestinian context. The logic of this criterion is self-evident: what Jesus said and did must make sense in a particular historical and cultural context. Unlike the other criteria, this one is used to argue against certain traditions as historically implausible. For example, the gospel of Thomas contains sayings that make perfect sense in the context of second-century gnosticism, but sound completely unlike what a first-century Jew in Palestine would have said. These things likely do not go back to Jesus. Another example is the discussion between Jesus and Nicodemus in John 3:3, in the saying about "being born from above," which Nicodemus understands to mean "being born again." That misunderstanding only makes sense in Greek, not in Aramaic, the language Jesus would have used. This criterion is particularly useful for understanding how Jesus understood himself and his role.

As we have seen, to understand Jesus, we must situate him in his own historical context. Jesus was a first-century Palestinian Jew, and as such lived in a period of foreign subjugation by Rome. One consequence of foreign subjugation of Palestine included the formation of Jewish sects such as the Sadducees and Pharisees, which exercised some power and offered religious options for Jews living at the time. The Essenes lived at the margins of society, maintaining their own purity through separation from institutional Judaism. Through unique lifestyle and fervent study of scripture, they lived in anticipation of the imminent apocalypse in which God would judge the world, thereby ending Roman rule and purifying Judaism. The Zealots emphasized Jewish autonomy and their divinely appointed duty to reestablish Israel as a sovereign state, by force if necessary.

Despite the somewhat favored treatment of Jews by Rome, Roman rule was nonetheless felt by many Palestinian Jews as an unbearable burden. Jews responded to Roman rule in a variety of ways, from silent protest to armed rebellion. During the first century CE, various Jewish prophets arose to speak against Rome as God's enemies and were often killed as troublemakers. One form of resistance ideology, apocalypticism, became prominent in the period. As we saw earlier, this ideology claimed that the forces of evil that were currently in charge of this world and responsible for its suffering would be overthrown by God in a mighty act of judgment. This imminent event was thought to be the prelude to the appearance of God's kingdom in a utopian age on earth. John the Baptist was an apocalyptic prophet of this sort, and we have compelling reasons for thinking that Jesus held such apocalyptic views.

Was Jesus an Apocalyptic Prophet?

The view that Jesus was an apocalypticist was first popularized by Albert Schweitzer in his 1906 classic text, *Quest of the Historical Jesus*. In this book Schweitzer showed how previous critical scholars had portrayed Jesus incorrectly, because they failed to recognize that he was an apocalypticist. When we examine our gospel sources critically, we find that Schweitzer was right. To understand Jesus correctly, it is important to follow a primary rule used by historians, namely, that we should prefer sources that are closest to the time of the events they narrate and that are not tendentious. In the case of Jesus, a clear perspective emerges when we examine the earliest sources at our disposal: Mark, Q, M (Mark's independent source), and L (Luke's independent source); all portray Jesus apocalyptically. Interestingly, later sources, such as John and the gospel of Thomas, do not.

In the earliest accounts of Jesus' teachings we find numerous apocalyptic predictions: a kingdom of God will soon appear on earth, in which God will rule. The forces of evil will be overthrown, and only those who repent and follow Jesus' teachings will enter the kingdom. Judgment on all others will be brought by the Son of Man, a cosmic figure who may arrive from heaven at any moment. Jesus is said to have proclaimed this message in all of our earliest surviving sources.

This is clearly the case in Mark 1:15 and 13:14–27, the latter passage ending with Jesus' proclamation: "Truly I tell you, this generation will not pass away until all these things have taken place" (Mark 13:30). The same message is found in Luke 17:24, 26–27 and Matthew 24:27, 37–39 (this is Q material), Matthew 13:40–43 (M), and Luke 21:34–36 (L). Some of these apocalyptic traditions are toned down in later traditions. For instance, contrast Mark 9:1 with Luke 9:27 and then with Luke 17:21 (found only in Luke). In this later gospel, Jesus no longer says that his disciples will see the kingdom come in power, but only that the kingdom will arrive in the ministry of Jesus. In Luke 17:21, Luke has Jesus state that the kingdom is "in your midst." This clearly differs from Mark's earlier "coming with power" (Mark 9:1).

The author of Luke's gospel does not seem to think that the coming of a real kingdom would occur in the lifetime of Jesus' companions. Evidently, because he was writing after they had died, and he knew that the end had not come, he deals with the "delay of the end" by making changes in Jesus' predictions. Later sources eliminate the apocalyptic material altogether. Thus, in the gospel of John, the kingdom is not described as imminent but as already present to those who believe in Jesus (3:3, 36). Here, in passages written near the end of the first century, the older apocalyptic idea that a day of judgment is coming and that the dead will be resurrected at the end of the historical age is replaced by a newer view, that in Jesus a person can already experience eternal life (11:23–26). This "de-apocalypticizing" of Jesus' message continues into the second century, as we see in the gospel of Thomas, which contains a clear attack on anyone who believes in a future kingdom on earth (sayings 3, 18, 118).

From this evidence a clear picture emerges. It appears that, when the expected end did not arrive, later Christians changed Jesus' message accordingly. However, when we examine the earliest sources, it is clear that Jesus was an apocalypticist. This certainly fits in with the specific criteria of contextual credibility, dissimilarity, and independent attestation. First-century Palestine had many apocalyptic Jews, some of whom left writings (such as the Essenes, who wrote the Dead Sea Scrolls). Other apocalyptic Jews were activists, including John the Baptist and prophets such as Theudas (see Acts 5:36-37) and "the Egyptian," mentioned by Josephus.

Some of the gospel references clearly pass the criterion of dissimilarity, such as Mark 8:38, in which Jesus talks about a cosmic judge of the earth (the Son of Man), without any suggestion that the reference is himself, even though early Christians did make this association, equating Jesus with the coming heavenly judge. That, however, is not what Jesus taught. In some cases he clearly did speak about himself using the term "son of man" (that is, son of a human), as a reference to his humanity, but when speaking about the future coming of the heavenly Son of Man, Jesus does not appear to have been speaking about himself.

Another passage that passes the criterion of dissimilarity is the parable of the sheep and goats in Matthew 25, which indicates that at the apocalyptic judgment, the Son of Man will judge the nations based on how they live. Since this does not coincide with the view of Jesus' later followers, who believed that salvation comes only on the basis of faith in Jesus and his resurrection, not on the basis of good works, the passage was likely not created by Christians but goes back to Jesus.

The tradition about Jesus as an apocalypticist also passes the criterion of independent attestation, since Jesus is portrayed thus in Mark, Q, M, and L but not in later sources, such as John or the second century gospel of Thomas. Each of those early sources are independent of one another and all portray Jesus apocalyptically.

In addition to meeting these criteria, one final piece of evidence seems convincing. Not only did Jesus begin his ministry apocalyptically, through association with the apocalyptic prophet John the Baptist, but his ministry concluded with apocalyptic Christian communities, such as those established by the apostle Paul, who believed he was living at the end of the age (see 1 Thess 4:13-5:10). If Jesus began his ministry as an apocalypticist, and if the first Christian communities were apocalyptic, then it seems most likely that the middle—Jesus' life and teaching—was also apocalyptic.

Jesus proclaimed that God's kingdom was coming to earth imminently (Mark 1:15). These words in Mark, the first words Jesus is recorded to have said in that gospel, provide a summary of Jesus' teaching. This would be a real kingdom with real rulers, a kingdom that would welcome some people but exclude others. Before the kingdom arrived, a scene of judgment would take place, in which the Son of Man, a cosmic figure from heaven, would appear to destroy God's enemies. This coming judgment would involve a massive reversal of fortunes; those who had prospered in this world through siding with evil would be displaced, but those who had suffered would be exalted. The judgment would come not only to individuals, but also to institutions and governments. In particular, the Jewish temple in Jerusalem, the heart of all institutional Jewish worship, would be destroyed.

Throughout his authentic teachings, when Jesus refers to the coming kingdom, he seems to mean an actual earthly kingdom, with actual rulers. Consider Jesus' teachings found in Q, perhaps our earliest source: "Truly I tell you, at the renewal of all things, when the Son of Man is seated on the throne of his glory, you who have followed me will also sit on twelve thrones, judging the twelve tribes of Israel" (Matt 19:28; cf. Luke 22:30). While the arrival of the kingdom was "good news" for Jesus' followers, it was not good news for everyone. In a mighty act of judgment, evil rulers would be toppled and punished, and the oppressed would be raised up (Luke 13:23–29; cf. Matt 8:11–12). This coming judgment would involve a serious reversal of fortune, one that makes sense in an apocalyptic context (Mark 10:31; Luke 13:30).

Likewise, Jesus' ethical teachings make best sense in an apocalyptic context. These teachings, however, have come down to us today as perfect examples of how people ought to live normally. Nevertheless, it is important for us to understand that the meaning of Jesus' ethical teachings might have been quite different in their original context from their meaning in ours. In our context, Jesus' teachings assist us in knowing how to get along with one another, so that we can contribute to a healthier and more wholesome society, allowing us to experience peace and wellbeing for the long haul. But for Jesus there was not going to be a long haul. The Son of Man would soon come in judgment, and people needed to prepare for entrance into his kingdom by showing that they sided with God rather than with the forces of evil that were opposed to him. Jesus' ethical teachings were ethics of the kingdom—they both reflected what life would be like in the kingdom and qualified one for entrance once it arrived.

In the kingdom, there would be no hatred; thus, people should love one another now. In the kingdom, there would be no oppression; thus, people should work for justice now. In the kingdom, there would be no war; thus, people should work for peace now. In the kingdom, there would be no sexism; thus, people should work for equality now. Only those who lived in ways that are appropriate to the kingdom would be allowed entrance when it arrived.

According to Jesus' teachings in the Sermon on the Mount, his followers should regard entrance into the kingdom as their most prized possession, and even be willing to give up all their possessions for the sake of the kingdom (Matt 6:25–33). Later on, Jesus indicates in his parable of the Pearl of Great Price (Matt 13:45–46) that the kingdom is like a merchant in search of fine pearls who finds a perfect pearl and then goes out and sells all that he has to buy it. The pearl is the kingdom, and it demands our ultimate allegiance; that's how valuable it is. For Jesus, nothing made sense apart from the kingdom of God that was on the verge of breaking into history. If its coming found one unprepared, all would be lost.

If Jesus' ethical teachings make best sense in an apocalyptic context, we need to rethink their meaning. Jesus, it appears, did not deliver timeless truths to guide individuals in leading long and productive lives. His teachings were meant to show people how to live in order to enter the kingdom that would soon appear. When we examine teachings such as "love your neighbor as yourself," and "love your enemies and pray for those who persecute you," he is teaching ethics of the coming kingdom. How else can we understand Jesus' teaching to the young ruler, that he should give up everything—all possessions and everything that binds one to this world (Mark 10:17–31)—except in this context? This emphasis on giving up everything for the kingdom means that Jesus was not a major proponent of what we now call "family values" (see Luke 14:26; 12:51–53). As with other hard sayings of Jesus, these should not be explained away so that they no longer mean what they say. Instead, they should be placed in an apocalyptic context.

Understood apocalyptically, Jesus' command to love one's neighbor and God above all else points to the coming kingdom, when God will provide such things as food and clothing (Matt 6:25–33). To those who trust God, all things are possible, for that is how God will care for us in his kingdom that is soon to come. Jesus, then, did not see himself as inventing a new system of ethics, so much as explaining the Law of Moses in view of his own apocalyptic context.

While later sources have Jesus proclaiming the kingdom as a present reality, this is not what Jesus actually taught. For him, the kingdom was imminent, but it had not yet arrived. Understanding Jesus' message of the coming judgment of the Son of Man, including the destruction of the temple in Jerusalem, helps explain Jesus' actions in the temple prior to his crucifixion. Viewed apocalyptically, they become a symbolic expression of his teaching, a prophetic gesture or enacted parable of the coming of

God's imminent judgment on the earth, beginning with institutional Judaism. In cleansing the temple, Jesus was demonstrating on a small scale what would soon occur in a large way.

Jesus was betrayed by one of his own followers, Judas Iscariot. What is not clear, though, is what it was that Judas betrayed, or why he acted as he did. Some believe that he betrayed Jesus for financial gain; others argue that Judas grew disillusioned when he realized that Jesus had no intention of becoming a political Messiah; yet still others have reasoned that Judas wanted to force Jesus' hand, thinking that if Jesus were arrested, he would call out for support and start an uprising that would overthrow the Romans. While each of these explanations has merit, the clearest explanation is that Judas may have divulged insider information that the authorities could use to bring Jesus up on charges. Jesus, it appears, taught his disciples things in private that he did not state publicly.

We have several hints as to what Jesus taught about himself that Judas might have divulged to the authorities. Almost certainly, the charge leveled against Jesus by the Roman governor Pontius Pilate was that he considered himself to be the King of the Jews (Mark 15:2; John 19:33; 19:19). However, Jesus never called himself this in any of the gospels. Why would he be executed for a claim he never made? Jesus did teach that after the Son of Man executed judgment on the earth, the kingdom would arrive. Kingdoms, by their nature, have kings. Who would be the king? Ultimately, of course, it would be God. However, Jesus probably did not think that God would physically sit on the throne in Jerusalem. Who, then, would?

The earliest traditions indicate that Jesus thought he would be enthroned. For one thing, only those who accepted his message would be accepted into the kingdom. Jesus also told his disciples that they would be seated on twelve thrones to rule the twelve tribes of Israel. Who would be over them? It was Jesus who had called them to be the Twelve. Moreover, his disciples asked him for permission to sit at his right hand and his left in the coming kingdom (Mark 10:37). Of course, the current textual context, as modified by later authors and redactors, changes the original meaning of Jesus' teaching. Rightly understood, his disciples would have viewed him as ruler in the kingdom, just as he was their "ruler" now.

Judas, then, betrayed this private teaching of Jesus to the Jewish authorities, and that explains why they could level the charges against Jesus that he called himself the Messiah, the King of the Jews. Of course, he meant it in the apocalyptic sense, but they meant it in a this-worldly sense. Once the local Jewish authorities learned this insider information, they had all the grounds they needed to make a quick arrest to get Jesus out of the public eye, and thus avoid any recriminations from their Roman overlords over disturbances caused by Jesus and his followers.

Questions for Discussion and Reflection

1. This chapter begins by discussing the pervasive influence of apocalyptic thinking upon Christians throughout history. In a sentence or two, define the word "apocalyptic." In your estimation, why have Christians been so attracted to this perspective?

2. In your estimation, are we living in the "last days"? Explain your answer.

3. Explain the origins of apocalyptic thinking in Judaism. In your estimation, what role did this perspective play in shaping the early Christian movement?

4. Modern scholarship is divided regarding Jesus' self-understanding. Some scholars view Jesus to be an apocalyptic prophet, whereas others envision a non-apocalyptic Jesus. Scholars such as Marcus Borg suggests alternative models said to accurately portray Jesus' self-understanding: mystic, healer, wisdom teacher, and social critic. It has become all too easy to see Jesus in one's own image. Some see him as a wandering Cynic, others as a feminist, and still others as social or political liberator. How do you view Jesus, apocalyptically or non-apocalyptically? Explain your answer.

5. Given the many additions and changes that entered the Jesus story in the decades prior to and during the recording of the gospels, scholars have devised three historical criteria to reconstruct the life and teachings of the historical Jesus. Explain these criteria and assess their merit. Which, if any, do you find most convincing? Explain your answer.

Chapter 10

The Historical Jesus and Apocalyptic Theology, Part II[1]

IT IS SAFE TO say that without the historical Jesus of Nazareth, there would be no Christian religion. It is equally certain that without belief in the resurrection of Jesus, the movement would hardly have gotten off the ground. Accompanying belief in Jesus' resurrection was the heartfelt liturgical cry, "He is alive!" Following the post-resurrection appearances—whether actual, visionary, or metaphorical[2]—and belief in the ascension of Jesus to heaven—whether bodily, spiritually, or metaphorically—there arose what later Christians called "the blessed hope" (Titus 2:13), a hope expressed as promise elsewhere throughout the New Testament and as a central conviction of the nascent Christian movement in the book of Acts (see 1:11). This anticipated return of Jesus would bring to earth God's promised kingdom, seen as the restoration of the kingdom to Israel, and bring human history to its climax, restoring all things to the pristine nature of their original creation. This Great Reversal of history was expected to happen very soon, probably within the lifetime of the first disciples and certainly within the lifetime of that first generation of believers (Mark 8:38—9:1; 13:24–27, 30).

---

1. This chapter continues the discussion begun in chapter 9.

2. According to New Testament scholar John Dominic Crossan, resurrection is "one of the metaphors used to express the sense of Jesus' continued presence with his followers and friends." *Who is Jesus?*, 121.

Jewish Eschatology and God's Millennial Reign

Belief in the return of Christ, known as the Second Coming, has long been the linchpin of Christian hope, the great expectation of all devout believers. Early on, it was connected with belief that Christ's return would usher in a millennial reign of God upon the earth. This belief, based upon a literal reading of an obscure passage in the biblical book of Revelation (20:1–10), was not an original concept with John of Patmos, the book's author, but was part of the tradition he inherited.[3]

I recall the day I heard with shock the report that certain biblical scholars were endorsing a view that the Second Coming had already occurred, a view said to be found in scripture itself. I was a student at a nondenominational Christian college, and my faith had yet to be tested. "How could anyone believe this?" I thought. It brought to mind a story my mother had told me, how she had encountered a similar surprise upon hearing that her former church, the Christian Reformed Church, affirmed a view called amillenialism, which taught that the millennial kingdom of God had already arrived and was to be equated with the historical church. Members of her family were beginning to attend a Baptist church, which took apocalyptic passages in the Bible literally. "How can we be in the millennium now?" her father questioned. "Doesn't the Bible say that during the millennium the devil will be bound? Do you think the devil is bound now?" he continued. My mother found she couldn't disagree with his reasoning, and from that moment she parted company with the church of her upbringing.

The book of Revelation is one of the most amazing depictions of Christian faith and life ever written; it is also divisive, having become the source of endless disputes and sectarian conflict. For generations, Revelation has tapped into some of people's deepest hopes but also their darkest fears. Sometimes the results have been spectacular and sometimes they have been tragic. A point we need to keep in mind has relevance to the assumptions we make about this book and to the questions we ask. If we assume that Revelation provides a literal outline of events leading up to the end of history, then we tend to view events described in the book as actual and as chronologically connected. From this perspective, material that appears early in the book precedes material found later in the book. Events described in chapter 20, for instance, would still be in the future,

---

3. A discussion of millennialism appears in appendix B, including four distinct positions Christians have taken on the meaning of the millennium.

and would occur at the very end of time, probably on earth, and immediately before the eschatological bliss. If we assume that the imagery in Revelation is symbolic in nature, then we focus on its meaning for John's original audience and for spiritual life in the present. In that case the timing of things—their interrelationship chronologically—diminishes into near irrelevance.

Revelation 20:1–10 is one of the most difficult passages in the entire book, the source of great contention and endless disputes, particularly among Protestant evangelicals. Revelation 20 introduces John's "double eschatology," one of the most mystifying scenarios in Revelation. After Satan's banishment he "must be let out for a little while" (20:3). To this point John has taken ideas from Jewish and Christian eschatology—the great banquet, the last battle, and the last judgment—and applied them to his own vision and understanding, indicating how he saw these expectations fulfilled. But then follows the millennium, and after the millennium an entirely new set of fulfillments of the same expectations: Gog and Magog are defeated in battle, the dead are judged, and the New Jerusalem descends from heaven like a bride adorned for her husband. Why would evil be defeated and banished, only to emerge again? One way to solve this dilemma is to downplay the concept of the millennium itself, regarding it as an item of traditional eschatology that John felt bound to include, although it played no integral part in his own thinking—it occurs only in this one passage in Revelation and nowhere else in the New Testament. But the concept does have validity for John, and would become vital to Christian apocalyptics throughout church history, particularly among Christian evangelicals in the nineteenth and twentieth centuries.

Revelation 20:4–10 bristles with questions. Why, for example, must Satan be loosed after having been securely sealed in the Abyss, and why the millennium? Why should the martyr church wait a thousand years for the bliss of the New Jerusalem? Who or what are Gog and Magog, and what part do they play in eschatology? And what is the first resurrection, and how does it relate to the second death? While answers to such questions are not germane to our discussion, we can say that they are based on two sources: the Jewish apocalyptic tradition, particularly that found in Ezekiel 37–39, and John's own theology of history.

For modern readers to comprehend this imagery, they need to understand that the millennial period at the end of history was not an original concept with John, but was a part of the tradition he inherited. The idea of a millennial period resulted from the combination of two different kinds of eschatology: (a) prophetic eschatology and (b) apocalyptic eschatology. *Prophetic eschatology* was essentially optimistic, tending to picture a this-worldly fulfillment of God's purpose at the end of history, when the world's evil would be overcome and when salvation (eschatological bliss), championed by an earthly Messiah, would emerge in continuity with history. In contrast, *apocalyptic eschatology* saw this world as too burdened with evil for redemption to occur from within. The present world must pass away to make way for eschatological fulfillment in the setting of new heavens and a new earth (Isa 65:17; 66:22; 2 Pet 3:12–13). In this conception, the Messiah is no earthly figure but a transcendent one that brings redemption from the other world. In apocalyptic eschatology, the final kingdom of God does not emerge out of this world but breaks into it from the beyond. "By John's time these two views had already been combined into a scheme in which a this-worldly messiah brought this-worldly salvation during a transitional kingdom, which was then superseded by eternal apocalyptic salvation in the new world."[4] The "two ages" were bridged by an intermediate period of messianic rule, a period varying from forty years to one thousand years.

According to the Epistle of Barnabas (a second century Christian writing), Jewish belief in a millennium had its origin in a combination of Genesis 2:2 and Psalm 90:4, whereby each of the seven days of creation becomes a thousand years of history, ending with the messianic Sabbath and succeeded by the timeless new world of the eighth day (this view is found in 2 Enoch 32:2–33:2, though without reference to the Messiah). The Apocalypse of Weeks (1 Enoch 91:12–17; 93) presents a similar perspective but divides world history into ten weeks of indeterminate length and singles out the seventh week as the period of apostasy. In 2 Esdras 7:28–30 the Messiah is expected to reign for four hundred years before dying along with the rest of his generation. In the Apocalypse of Elijah (261 CE), in many ways resembling Revelation, the age of the Messiah is to last only forty years. In other Jewish writings, such as the Similitudes of Enoch (1 Enoch 37–71), there is no earthly kingdom intervening before the transformation of heaven and earth.

John adopts this picture partly because he stands in this tradition but also because he is influenced here as elsewhere by the storyline of Ezekiel. The "first resurrection" and millennial period (20:4–6) corresponds to Ezekiel 37, the defeat of God and Magog (20:7–10) to Ezekiel 38–39, and

---

4. Boring, *Revelation*, 206–7.

the coming of the Holy City (21:1–22:5) to Ezekiel 40–48. In addition, John inherits from his Jewish background the tradition that only the just are raised (Isa 26:19) and the tradition that all the dead, good and bad alike, are raised (Ezek 37; Dan 12:2–3). By adopting the scheme of an intermediate eschatological period, he discovers a conceptual means of affirming both traditions. It was the Jewish tradition that provided the elements for John's conception, but his own vision that provided the additional features.

In the Bible, teaching concerning salvation and the afterlife is very much a part of its eschatological perspective. Eschatology is the study of final things, including the resurrection of the dead, the Last Judgment, the defeat of evil, the end of this world, and the creation of a new world. A fully formed eschatology with all of these features emerged only late in the development of biblical traditions.

The classic prophets of Israel were mostly concerned with the events of history, speaking boldly and without compromise against current disobedience and disbelief within the social, religious, and political establishment. Biblical prophets rarely, if ever, made open predictions about the future, and when they did so, the predictions were linked to their role as social critics, which focused on the consequences for unrepentance. The prophet's futuristic role was associated primarily with the certainty of the coming of the Lord, a coming to make things right through judgment and reward.

Toward the end of the sixth century BCE, after the Jews returned from the Babylonian captivity, they held on to the prophetic hopes and visions, longing for a time when they could function once again under theocratic ideals. During the postexilic period, the prophetic expectation expanded to include messianic hope. However, the kingdom of God did not materialize, and messianic hope was deferred.

As time went on, some persecuted members of the Jewish community became pessimistic about an earthly kingdom of God and looked for salvation from above through direct intervention from God. This led to the development of apocalyptic eschatology, found in postexilic passages added to the book of Isaiah, dubbed the Isaianic apocalypse (Isa 24–27), and Third Isaiah (Isa 56–66). These passages speculate about end-time events, including the Lord's arrival as king on Mount Zion, the judgment of the nations accompanied by heavenly portents, the abolition of death, the resurrection of the dead, the destruction of Leviathan (the chaos monster), and the creation of a new heaven and a new earth.

Like the prophets, apocalyptists expected an end followed by a new era of God's saving activity. But the apocalyptists saw the end as complete and final. The judgment would be not only on Israel but on all nations. This judgment would include not only their earthly foes but the cosmic forces of evil as well. Many of these elements appear in the New Testament, for early Christianity inherited its eschatological framework from Judaism.

Jesus and the Presence of the Kingdom

The dominant theme in the preaching of Jesus—indeed the center of his mission and message—is the coming of the kingdom of God. While the phrase "kingdom of God" is rare in contemporary Jewish writings, it is widely regarded as one of the most distinctive aspects of the preaching of Jesus. Because almost everywhere in the Old Testament the idea of the kingdom is related to the people of Israel and the rule of the house of David in Jerusalem, Jesus is at pains to divest his teaching of this former understanding of the nature of the kingdom. What Jesus proclaims is the immediate sovereignty of God, who will take control of the destinies of all humans, restore humanity to what God had intended it to be, and overthrow the evil powers that had led astray human beings from their proper destiny.

In Mark's gospel, Jesus' first act upon returning from his sojourn in the wilderness is to proclaim the coming of the kingdom (1:15). Here Jesus picks up where Second Isaiah (Isa 40–55) left off half a millennium earlier. Isaiah had envisioned a day when God would finally bring justice to the world, when the long-suffering faithful could rejoice at the end of oppression. Jesus shared Isaiah's anticipation but was more specific about when this time would come: "Truly I tell you, there are some standing here who will not taste death until they see that the kingdom of God has come with power" (Mark 9:1). His audience was to repent and "believe in the good news."

Whatever Jesus envisioned in his proclamation about the kingdom, it was going to be on earth. Despite Matthew's preference for the expression, "kingdom of heaven," it is clear that the concept, as Jesus used it, refers to the destiny of good people on a new, improved earth. It has nothing to do with the souls of dead people ascending to heaven.

In New Testament teaching, the coming of the kingdom is always dependent on divine initiative, never on human achievement. Humans may enter the kingdom; they may proclaim it and inherit it (Matt 25:34; 7:21), but they can neither earn it nor bring it forth. Because the word "kingdom" suggests a geographical region or realm, which is misleading in this context, scholars prefer the term "kingship" or "kingly rule of God."

The term "kingdom" is complex and paradoxical at its core. In the synoptic gospels, the paradoxical nature of the kingdom is manifested in several ways: (a) it is present (Matt 12:28; Luke 17:21), yet not fully present (Matt 8:29; 13:30); (b) it is a gift (Matt 25:34; Luke 12:32), yet it also involves human effort (Matt 6:33; Luke 12:31); (c) it is an internal reality (Luke 17:20–21), yet it has external implications for the world (Matt 6:10). Scholars are particularly interested in the first of these, for it addresses the tension between the present time and the future, the "already" and the "not yet." In that regard, they have introduced the term "inaugurated eschatology" to refer to the relation of the present inauguration and the future fulfillment of the kingdom.

There is a present element in the New Testament concept of the kingdom, particularly in the teaching of Jesus, which is colored by a sense of intense urgency. God has already taken the initiative; humans are challenged to recognize the reality of the present situation and to make such decisions as will qualify them to become citizens of the kingdom. The signs of the presence of the kingdom are already present in the ministry of Jesus. When John the Baptist questions the mission of Jesus and asks for signs, he is given clear evidence: "the blind receive their sight, the lame walk, the lepers are cleansed, the deaf hear, the dead are raised, and the poor have good news brought to them" (Matt 11:5). All these are signs that the power of the kingdom is presently at work. Those who refuse to recognize that the power evident in Jesus is a power from God are told: "if it is by the finger of God that I cast out the demons, then the kingdom of God has come to you" (Luke 11:20). When one person, for a period of some thirty-five years, lives in total dependence upon God, with a unique understanding of God's will and in unconditional surrender to it, the kingdom is already present. As Jesus tells the Pharisees in answer to their question about when the kingdom was coming: "the kingdom of God is among you" (Luke 17:21).

According to the New Testament, Christians are kind of hybrid creatures who live in two dimensions. They are citizens of the present age while at the same time living under the dominion of Christ's kingdom.

As Paul put it somewhat paradoxically, Christians live "in the flesh" (human nature) and also "in the Spirit" (the new dimension introduced by Christ). Awareness of this dual citizenship led early Christians to say that they were "strangers" in the historical era on earth (Heb 11:13).

Ever since the New Testament period, Christianity has had to steer between two dangers: the temptation (1) to withdraw from society on the assumption that Christ's kingdom is not of this world (John 18:36), and (2) to make a too easy identification of the kingdom with something in this world, such as the institutional church or the ideal human society. However, the essential message of the New Testament is this: The kingdom is not of this world, yet it has been manifest in this world through the life, death, and resurrection of Christ. Although God's kingdom is a higher order than any political reality or human ideal of the present age, it has influenced and penetrated the kingdoms of this world—not as a tangent touches a circle but as a vertical line intersects a horizontal plane. The task of the church is to bear witness to this "vertical dimension" of history and, in so doing, to seek to leaven and redeem society in the name of Christ. This attitude toward society is not one of "detachment" but of "transfiguration," involving a rhythm of withdrawal and return through worship and action, faith and good works.

The tension between the "already" and the "not yet" nature of the kingdom is evident also in Paul's eschatology. At several points Paul emphasizes that the coming of Jesus inaugurates a new era or "age," which he designates a "new creation" (2 Cor 5:17). While the presence of this new age can already be experienced, for Paul the ultimate transformation of the world is yet to come. Viewing the resurrection of Jesus as eschatological event, for it confirms that the "new age" is truly present, Paul also looks ahead to the future coming of Jesus Christ in judgment at the end of time. Another theme of Paul's eschatology is the coming of the Holy Spirit. This theme, which builds on a long-standing aspect of Jewish expectation, sees the gift of the Spirit as a confirmation that the new age has dawned in Christ. One of the most significant aspects of Paul's thought is his interpretation of the gift of the Spirit to believers as a "guarantee" or "first installment" of ultimate salvation (2 Cor 1:22; 5:5).

To understand Jesus and the gospels, scholars suggest three eschatological perspectives: (1) "consistent eschatology," meaning that Jesus' eschatological teachings as presented in the gospels refer only to what will happen at the end of the world; (2) "realized eschatology," meaning that Jesus understood the anticipated kingdom of God to have arrived with himself; and (3) "inaugurated eschatology," meaning that Jesus brought the dawning of the awaited kingdom. This latter view finds some aspects of God's reign to be present in Jesus, but other elements of the kingdom would not appear until the very end. It is clear from passages such as the Synoptic Apocalypse (see Mark 13; Matt 24–25; and Luke 21), where signs of the end are given, that Jesus believed the fullness of the kingdom would arrive shortly, probably within his generation (see Mark 13:30).

For the writers of the New Testament, Jesus' followers are situated between the inauguration of the kingdom of God and its consummation. In the meantime, they are to be busy preaching the gospel, doing good works, and modeling exemplary lives.

The Kingdom of God–Then and Now

During the COVID-19 pandemic, described by American filmmaker Ken Burns as possibly the worst calamity to befall our country—equal if not greater than the Civil War, the Great Depression, and World War II—people began using the word "apocalyptic" to describe the fallout. Often, this word is used to scare people into some kind of fearful attitude, generally associated with the expectation of the "end times." However, the word "apocalyptic," from the Greek *apokalupsis*, simply means "unveiling."

Apocalyptic literature "pulls back the curtain" to reveal what is real, true, and lasting. This is the gift not only of this literature but also of the painful experiences of our time. Apocalyptic literature shocks us out of what we take for granted as normal and helps us to see more clearly the purpose of life. It uses hyperbolic language and imagery such as stars falling from the sky and the metaphor of the moon turning to blood to awaken us from our comfort zones and to help us recognize cataclysmic change. While apocalyptic imagery originally pointed to the end of the world, today it helps us to rethink the end of our world as we know it. This doesn't mean that life doesn't continue, only that our lives won't go the way we thought they would, could, or even should. Apocalyptic thinking allows us to let go of previous securities and boundaries that no longer work or appear relevant.

When reality is "unveiled," we stop taking things for granted. That is what life-changing events like the COVID-19 pandemic do for us. They reframe reality in a radical way and offer us an invitation to greater depth and breadth. If we trust the universal patterns, the wisdom of all times and places, including the creation and the evolution of the cosmos, we know that endings are but new beginnings, and that deaths bring about newness of life.

When Jesus came, life was bleak for Jews; Rome was dominant, brutal, and aggressive. In declaring that the temple would be destroyed,[5] Jesus assumed the end of institutional Judaism and the destruction of Jerusalem. Why? Because it was the end? Not necessarily. While the coming of the kingdom announces the end of old beliefs, patterns, and securities, it also marks the beginning of the new. As Christian millennialism makes clear, the kingdom is about new beginnings, about restoration and regeneration. With the cessation of the old come new beginnings.

Was Jesus a failed apocalyptic prophet, as John Loftus and others have claimed? Was Christianity simply an offshoot of "the Jesus cult movement," one additional group of deceived people following another failed doomsday prophet?[6] I don't believe so. Did Jesus believe in the coming of an imminent divine kingdom to earth, which would overthrow current rulers, empower the poor and lowly, and end history as we know it? Yes, he did. But his conviction was part of a larger vision, for the coming kingdom was more than about endings. It was about new beginnings. Jesus knew that society cannot have a new start without a powerful, comprehensive ending. As a prophet, he was more than a visionary. He was a person of hope.

However we understand him, Jesus was a Stage Four individual, and hence, a transformative leader. Unlike one-dimensional leaders, he was a person of unusual wisdom and spirituality. If he was an apocalyptic prophet, he was a Stage Four apocalyptic prophet, with power to transform the world. A man for all seasons, he could be trusted to lead people through all stages of faith.

Jesus didn't limit his thinking to belief in a glorious future, with its new world. Rather, he brought the doctrine into the present, living out of the resources of the future proleptically. This is why scholars label his teachings "realized eschatology" or "inaugurated eschatology." As later Christians went on to claim, God's kingdom is present here and now (Luke 17:21); eternal life is a present reality (John 3:36; 6:47); abundant life is available now (John 10:10).

---

5. See Mark 13:2; also 14:58; 15:29; something similar is independently stated in John 2:19 and in the gospel of Thomas: "I will destroy this house and no one will be able to rebuild it," saying 71.

6. Loftus, *Christian Delusion*, 317.

Accepting the goodness of God's creation, as well as the damage caused by human pride and interference, Jesus came to offer new possibilities. Believing in the power of the Jesus story to transform society, Brian McLaren, together with Gareth Higgins, tells how Jesus came to subvert all stories of violence and harm.[7] Exposing and delegitimizing stories of domination, Jesus taught and embodied service, reconciliation, and self-giving. Instead of stories of violent revolution, revenge, or of compliant submission, he taught and modeled transformative nonviolent resistance. Instead of purification stories of scapegoating or ethnic cleansing, he engaged strangers and aliens with respect, welcome, neighborliness, and mutuality. Instead of competitive stories of accumulation, he advocated stewardship, generosity, sharing, and a vision of abundance for all. Instead of apocalyptic stories of isolation and escapism, he sent his followers into the world to be agents of positive change. And instead of leaving the oppressed in stories of victimization, he empowered them with a vision of faith, hope, and love that could change the world.

Those six stories of violence and harm all claimed that the path to peace, security, and happiness was about "winning." However, in the Jesus Story, the story of reconciliation and love, humans still get to win, only not at anyone else's expense. In the Seventh Story, human beings are not the protagonists of the world. Love is.[8]

For people of faith, the kingdom brings Faith Stages One, Two, and Three to an end in order to make way for the emergence of Stage Four living and thinking. Known as the second half of life, this way of "living into a new way of thinking" brings death to the controlling, manipulative ego, and makes possible the resurrection of the True Self. This newness cannot be experienced without letting go of the possessive old self, with its old ways and former beliefs.

Doctrines such as the incarnation, the Virgin Birth, the atonement, the transfiguration, the resurrection, and the ascension of Jesus, and apocalyptic beliefs such as the Second Coming and the millennium should not be abandoned as lies, fake news, or delusions. Rather, they are the language of myth, a central characteristic of biblical literature. When the Bible speaks of the eternal boundaries of the human drama, it does so metaphorically, in the language of myth. Keep in mind that the term "myth," understood literarily, does not refer to something purely

---

7. McLaren and Higgins, *Seventh Story*.
8. McLaren and Higgins, *Seventh Story*, 38, 40–42.

fictitious, but rather is a way of thinking that transcends reason. Scholars of religion often use the term "myths" to refer to the central narratives of a religious tradition, insisting that the term does not imply judgment either for or against the historicity or validity of the narratives.

Central religious myths manifest the character of the cosmic order and our relationship to it. Significant in personal and communal life because they endorse particular ways of ordering experience, myths provide exemplary patterns for human actions, individually and communally. Mythology, Karen Armstrong reminds us, "is not about opting out of this world, but about enabling us to live more intensely within it."[9]

What Would Jesus Do?

Some years ago, it was fashionable for evangelical Christians and even for non-Christians to wear a bracelet with the letters WWJD, an abbreviation of "What Would Jesus Do?" The motto became popular in the United States in the late 1800s, after the publication of the widely read book by Charles Sheldon titled *In His Steps: What Would Jesus Do?* The phrase had a resurgence in the 1990s as a personal reminder for adherents of Christianity to live faithfully.

While adherence to Christian social and ethical values is commendable, it is based on a questionable premise, that we can know how a first-century Jewish mystic named Jesus might think and act in the twenty-first century. While the rationale behind this WWJD motto is based on the notion that Jesus' deeds and thought process are captured reliably in the four gospels of the New Testament, that motive is radically flawed, for the gospels reflect more the ethical and theological views and interpretations of second and third generation Christians than verbatim conversations, sermons, and factual eyewitness accounts.

For the authors of Matthew, Luke, and John, certainly, Jesus was primarily a divine being with certain human qualities, but not truly human at all. In these writings, the words and actions of Jesus are viewed through the authors' christological lens. For Mark, the first gospel writer, Jesus was born human but exalted to divine sonship at his baptism.

Before we moderns try to imitate Jesus' behavior, we must address two preliminary questions, acknowledging that neither can be answered definitively:

9. Armstrong, *Short History of Myth*, 3.

1. Was the historical Jesus human or divine? If he was fully human, he was like us in every respect, and his ethical motivation and behavior would be relevant and imitable. If he was fully divine, then his motivation and behavior would ultimately be irrelevant and unattainable to fallible, mortal creatures.
2. If Jesus were alive in the twenty-first century, what would Jesus do? How would he behave, and what would his motivating values be?

If Jesus taught and lived as an apocalyptic Jewish prophet in the twenty-first century, few if any Christians would follow him. Nevertheless, most Christians follow him as a first-century apocalyptic Jew. How ironic!

Was Jesus literally born of a virgin? Of course not. Did he literally walk on water, multiply food, or turn water into wine? I sincerely doubt it. Was he literally raised bodily from the dead? Not if he was fully human. Did he literally die for our sins? Only if we believe in animal sacrifices as vicarious atonement, something most of us neither believe nor practice. What, then, does it mean to follow Jesus?

I believe there is no more important topic for inquiry today than the meaning and message of Jesus, no more important concern than one's answer to Jesus' perennial question, "Who do you say that I am?" (Mark 8:29), for in this quest, I believe, lies the solution to individual malaise and humanity's woes.

Questions for Discussion and Reflection

1. Without belief in Jesus' resurrection from the dead, it is safe to say that Christianity would have been just another failed messianic movement. What role did belief in the general resurrection of humanity from the dead play in apocalyptic theology?
2. Explain the doctrine of the Second Coming of Christ. In your estimation, how did this belief arise?
3. While apocalyptic passages are scattered across the New Testament, the book of Revelation is its sole example of apocalyptic literature. What role has this book played throughout Christian history, and how has it contributed to Christian eschatology?

4. What do Christians mean by the "millennium," and what role does this concept play in modern evangelical theology? *Note*: the appendix provides an overview of modern millennial views.

5. In your estimation, how are the Christian doctrines of salvation and the afterlife associated with the apocalyptic perspective?

6. In your estimation, what do Christians mean by the phrase "the kingdom of God"? How do popular notions of God's kingdom differ from what Jesus taught and believed about God's kingdom?

7. Explain the distinction between "consistent eschatology," "realized eschatology," and "inaugurated eschatology."

8. If Jesus were to appear in our midst today, what would he want us to know about his nature and his mission?

Chapter 11

Christianity after Religion

WHEN WE THINK ABOUT the history of religion in America, it is customary to speak of reform, revivals, and Awakenings, and to distinguish between three or possibly four Great Awakenings. The First Great Awakening (c. 1730–1760) marked the end of European styles of church organization and created an experiential, democratic community of faith called evangelicalism. The Second Great Awakening (c. 1800–1830) ended Calvinist theological dominance and initiated new understandings of free will that resulted in a voluntary system for church membership and benevolence work. Historians have described this awakening as an Americanization of religion.

The Second Awakening led to the Social Gospel movement, with its progressive politics; the Pentecostal movement, with an emphasis on miraculous transformation; and nonconformist movements like the Jehovah's Witnesses, the Seventh-Day Adventists, and Christian Science. The Jehovah's Witnesses, founded by Charles Taze Russell (1852–1916), focus on concepts like the Second Coming of Christ, the end of the world, and the establishment of God's millennial kingdom on earth. The Seventh-Day Adventists, initially inspired by the predictions of William Miller (1782–1849)—who erroneously announced that Christ would return to earth in 1843, later revised to October 22, 1844—are guided by the visions of Ellen White (1827–1915), who combined millennial expectation with an emphasis upon the seventh-day, or Saturday, as the correct Sabbath for Christians. Christian Science, founded by Mary Baker Eddy (1829–1910), while reflecting neither the teachings of Christianity nor the principles of science, built upon the prestige of Christianity and science to advance an alternative view of healing that emphasizes the power of religion in health and wellbeing.

During each Awakening, old patterns of religious life gave way to new ones, spawning new organizational forms that focused on revitalizing social, economic, and political life. Some writers say America is experiencing a Fourth Great Awakening (c. 1960–present), using terms such as postmodern, emerging (or emergent), and convergence to define it. Because this Awakening is affecting all religion in America, not just American Protestantism as in the past, it might be better described as the Fourth Great Awakenings (plural). The distinguished Harvard theologian Harvey Cox described this multireligious awakening as the Age of the Spirit, a widespread, experiential, practice-centered spiritual impulse sweeping across the globe. With such scope, it may not be the "Fourth" of anything, but rather the Great Global Awakening, the first of its kind. Whether the "age of belief" has ended, as Cox suggests, or the new has begun, as William McLoughlin proposed in his influential book *Revivals, Awakenings, and Reform* (1978), this latest Awakening, said to be occurring in the present, is long-lasting, in part because it is viewed to have unfolded in two distinctive periods (1960–1980 and 1995–present), with an interlude in between.[1]

The first phase, unfolding during the 1960s and 1970s, was a time of dramatic change, characterized as progressive, countercultural, pluralistic, and antiauthoritarian. As a result, two forms of evangelical religion emerged in the 1970s and 1980s: (1) romantic evangelicalism, an experiential, internally driven faith, and (2) dogmatic evangelicalism, a belief-centered, externally driven faith. The first, inclusive by nature, embraced newness and change; the second, exclusive, authoritarian, and nativist by nature, focused on stability and conservatism.

What happened religiously during the interlude between these two phases is quite stunning, including an increase in the number of Americans who claimed no religious affiliation (the number nearly doubled between 1990 and 2009, rising from 8 to 15 percent). In addition, the percentage of self-identified Christians fell 10 points during this period, from 86 to 76 percent, while the percentage of people who claimed they were unaffiliated of any particular religion doubled, rising to 16 percent. Furthermore, during that period, the number of people who described themselves as atheist or agnostic increased almost fourfold, from 1 million to 3.6 million.

---

1. Bass, *Christianity After Religion*, 241.

What characterized the first phase of this Fourth Awakening is that all sorts of people—even mature, faithful Christians—were finding conventional religion increasingly less satisfying. However, despite attending church less regularly, they longed for new expressions of spiritual community. McLoughlin characterized his Fourth Awakening as a "Romantic" awakening of experiential, quest-oriented, and self-aware religion. This emerging spirituality was grounded in a new social vision, for it included a profound commitment to justice, pluralism, freedom, and inclusive democracy. Other analysts dubbed this movement the "Next Christendom," claiming that America was witnessing the most significant change in the Christian faith since the Protestant Reformation. Traditional Christians watched from the sidelines, perplexed at the unfolding drama of this paradigm shift.

What characterizes the belief-driven second phase of this Fourth Awakening, particularly 2010 to the present, is a nativist religio-political movement that began with the strong backlash against President Obama known as the Tea Party. It was concretized and revitalized by President Trump under the slogan "Make America Great Again" (MAGA), a movement like the one described by William McLoughlin of reactionaries who look backward to a golden time, when the system worked; they insist that it will still work if only everyone confesses to the old standards.

Fear is still a powerful motivator, and the good old days seem good to those caught in a web of economic change, collapsing industries, and social insecurity. Many people in groups such as the Tea Party and the MAGA movement are devout believers in God, their families, and their country. Reactionary believers often support paths of authority and order in days that seem unhinged. To them, complete conformity to a singular interpretation of the Bible is the only way to happiness and salvation.

Yet coercion and fear are never compassionate. In the past, periods of intense social change and periods of intense religious encounters between different faiths often resulted in historical tragedies when fear-based religious groups gained political power. We live in a time of religious warfare, not just between different religions, but rather, in a dangerous time of intrareligious warfare, between those with differing versions of the same faith. During the Trump presidency, the nativists returned with fury. This version of religious and political hatred has been described by observers as the worst in American history since the Civil War. The current mood in our country does not bode well for the future. Theologian Harvey Cox calls it the fundamentalist rearguard action of those clinging to "belief-centered" faith, the fearful opposition to this global Age of the Spirit. According to Diana Bass, nativists of all sorts are doing their best to halt the spiritual awakening of romantic realism, bent on undoing the future it might create.[2] Ironically, the global spiritual awakenings of hope and possibility have created global nativist movements of fear and dread: fear of spiritual change but also of economic, political, and social change.

The concept of "awakenings" is controversial and much debated, due in part to its multifaceted nature; the difficulty distinguishing between religious change, reform, and awakening; and the inability to date these movements with precision. Focusing on current shifts in Christian belief and practice, we begin by distinguishing between the terms "religious" and "spiritual." What do these terms mean, and how are they distinct?

For much of Western history, the words meant roughly the same thing: how humans relate with God through rituals, practices, and communal worship. However, the popular meaning of the words diverged during the twentieth century. The word "spiritual" gradually came to be associated with the private realm of thought and experience, while the word "religious" came to be connected with the public realm of membership in religious institutions, participation in formal ritual, and adherence to official denominational doctrines. In general, "spirituality" came to take a positive and attractive meaning, as somehow more authentic, whereas "religious" took on a more negative connotation. In the mind of traditionalists, however, the term "spirituality" suggested something vague or vacuous, lacking substance and consistency. Spirituality, however, is neither vague nor meaningless. While it lacks precision, the word "spiritual" is both a critique of institutional religion and a longing for meaningful correction. The following partial list helps distinguish these categories.

Spirituality	*Religion*
experience	institution
searching	order
intuition	dogma
open	defined
wisdom	principles
inclusive	boundaries
doubt	certainty

---

2. Bass, *Christianity After Religion*, 250.

In recent studies, religious pollsters in a number of countries have begun asking people whether they consider themselves "spiritual but *not* religious . . . religious but *not* spiritual . . . religious *and* spiritual . . . or *not* spiritual and *not* religious." The most surprising result is to the first option. In the United States, 30 percent of adults selected this option. In Canada, 40 percent selected this choice, and in England, as many as 51 percent state they understand themselves in this way. In 2009, Princeton Survey Research Associates found that only 9 percent of Americans considered themselves "religious but not spiritual," while some 48 percent viewed themselves as "religious and spiritual." The World Values Survey, associated with the University of Michigan, found that in many developed nations, as high as 70 percent of the population self-defined as "generalized spirituality in contrast to traditional religions."[3] As these polls demonstrate, the word "spiritual" is far more appealing in post-Christian societies than the term "religious."

In her seminars across the United States, Diana Bass discovered that only 6 percent of the attendees self-identify as "religious only," 20 percent say they are "spiritual but not religious," while 72 percent of those who claim affiliation with a religious denomination consider themselves "spiritual and religious."[4]

While most Americans see themselves as "being religious" and "being spiritual," this has not always been the case. As recently as 1999, Gallup polled Americans asking whether they considered themselves to be spiritual or religious. At that time, 54 percent of the respondents answered "religious only," while only 6 percent answered "both spiritual and religious." Only ten years later, a *Newsweek* poll showed 9 percent answering "religious only," while 48 percent answered "both spiritual and religious." In both cases, the figures for "spiritual only" (30 percent) and "neither spiritual nor religious" (9 percent) remained the same.

What accounts for the significant change in the first two categories? What caused such a drastic shift in self-designation? While any number of factors might account for the change, the key to this discontent is found in the ten short years between 2000 and 2010, a period dubbed the "horrible decade." During that period, religious affiliation plummeted across the breadth of Christian denominations, while interest in spirituality grew.

3. Bass, *Christianity After Religion*, 66.
4. Bass, *Christianity After Religion*, 92.

What happened in the United States during the first decade of the twenty-first century was not good for religion as a whole, not just for Christian congregations or denominations. In particular, five major events revealed the ugly side of organized religion, leading to a "participation crash" across the religious spectrum. Diana Bass lists these as follows:

1. 2001: The September 11 terrorist attacks (despite a month or two of increased church attendance following the attacks, suddenly, without much fanfare, people stopped going to church)
2. 2002: the Roman Catholic sex abuse scandal
3. 2003: Protestant conflict over homosexuality
4. 2004: The Religious Right wins the battle, but loses the war (while the second election of George W. Bush in 2004 proved to be a great victory for conservative evangelical religion, it also alienated an entire generation of young people)
5. 2007: The Great Religious Recession (despite religious growth and optimism in the late 1990s, the early 2000s saw a significant drop in public trust in religious institutions. The economic recession of 2007 arrived at a moment when churches and denominations were in significant decline. The economic crisis did not drive people to religion; instead, it drove religion farther into irrelevance).[5]

By 2015, the phenomenon of shrinking faith communities became so widespread that "nones" (that is, the unaffiliated) became the third-largest religious identity in the world (16 percent), behind Christians (31 percent) and Muslims (23 percent), and just ahead of Hindus (15 percent).[6] And more Americans are joining the ranks of the religiously unaffiliated. Today there are more religious "nones" than Catholics or evangelicals, and 36 percent of those born after 1981 don't identify with any religion.

As it turns out, the current problem is not just a religious problem but also a human problem. In the absence of religion, fractious humans are simply uniting and dividing around other things: ideologies, dictators, demagogues, racial identities, wealth, weaponry, patriotism, conspiracy theories, revenge, and hate groups. If human beings don't consolidate and

---

5. Bass, *Christianity After Religion*, 76–83.
6. April 2, 2015 Pew forum; cited in McLaren, *Faith After Doubt*, 109.

unite, antagonistic individuals and nations will sooner or later press the red button and nuclear weapos will fly. And they will quickly discover that radiation does not discriminate between Christian, Muslim, atheist, or humanist flesh. Whether the bombs fall in the name of God, race, nation, revenge, or economic ideology, there will be no winners when civilization self-destructs.

Less dramatic but no less catastrophic, ego- and money-driven individuals and corporations will keep plundering the earth, risking the long-term health of all life on earth for short-term returns for their corporate investors. Rising sea levels, hurricanes, wildfires, and droughts won't discriminate between black or white lives, Christian or Muslim lives, rich or poor lives, socialist or capitalist lives, even between "nones" and the religiously minded. None of this will matter to a destabilized ecosystem.

Ultimately, we need radical change in each sector of life, flowing from a new set of values and deeper spiritual narratives. And we need forward-leaning faith communities to nourish those values and narratives in the context of a new kind of faith, a faith characterized by humility rather than arrogance, solidarity with the other rather than exclusion and antagonism, courage rather than fear, collaboration rather than competition, and love rather than self-interest.

The End of the Beginning

If the end of older forms of Christianity began in the 1960s and 1970s, now, decades later, we might be witnessing the end of that beginning. In describing the current New Awakening, Diana Bass speaks of a Great Returning to the origins of religions, when religion and spirituality were co-terminal. Utilizing a distinction made by Wilfred Cantwell Smith, a Harvard professor of comparative religion, in his 1962 book *The Meaning and End of Religion*, Bass points out that the end of religion, as currently defined, is not necessarily a bad thing, for the contemporary concept of "religion" is a relatively recent invention in European history. Christian writers began using the term "religion" during the seventeenth century to signify a system of ideas or beliefs about God. But that is not the original meaning of the word religion or of its Latin root *religio*. Unlike religion as a system of belief, *religio* signified the awe that human beings felt in the presence of the unknown. It included a response to a subjective experience, an attitude of trust and reverence toward the divine or toward nature. As something within one's heart, *religio* involved a path of wonder through the wilderness of change and uncertainty.

For Bass, what is ending and what needs to end is the modern Western understanding of religion, not its original subjective, intuitive, passionate dimension. What we have seen in recent times, not only in the West but also globally, is a turning from religion and a return to *religio*, only it is being called "spirituality," since no other English term conveys the new religious sensibility. The awakening taking place today is not an evangelical revival; nor is it a returning to the faith of our ancestors. Instead, "it is a Great Returning to ancient understandings of the human quest for the divine . . . . *Religio* is never satisfied with old answers, codified dogmas, institutionalized practices, or invested power. *Religio* invites every generation to experience God—to return to the basic questions of believing, behaving, and belonging—and explore each anew with an open heart."[7]

Taking three concepts—believing, behaving, and belonging—in the order of their centrality and importance to institutional religion, Bass offers an alternative, which she calls "the Great Reversal." For the last few centuries, Western Christianity ordered faith in a certain way. Catholics and Protestants taught that belief came first, behavior (ethics) came next, and finally belonging resulted, depending on how one affirmed the first two categories. Churches turned this pattern into rituals of catechism, character formation, and confirmation.

However, it was not always this way. The pattern found in early Christianity, certainly in the first Christian records, indicates that long ago, before the church councils of the first half millennium and before Christianity split into competing families of faith, each defending itself against the other, faith was a matter of community first, practices second, and belief third. Our immediate ancestors reversed the order, and it is up to us to restore the original order: belonging, behaving, and believing.

According to Bass, "Christianity of the Great Returning is the oldest-time religion—reclaiming a faith where belief is not quite the same thing as an answer, where behavior is not following a list of dos and don'ts, and where belonging to Christian community is less like joining an exclusive club and more of a relationship with God and others."[8] Relational community, intentional practice, and experiential belief are forming a new

---

7. Bass, *Christianity After Religion*, 99.
8. Bass, *Christianity After Religion*, 99.

vision for what it means to be Christian in the twenty-first century, a pattern of spiritual awakening that is growing around the world. We belong to God and to one another, connected to all in a web of relationships, and there we find our truest selves. The Great Reversal is the Great Returning of Christianity toward what Jesus preached: a beloved and belonging community, a way of life practiced in the world, and a profound trust in God that eagerly affirms God's present reign of mercy and justice.

Questions for Discussion and Reflection

1. Define the term "religious Awakening." How many Awakenings have scholars identified in America to date? When have they occurred, and what changes did they bring to society and to American Christianity?
2. Describe and assess the emerging spirituality during the so-called Fourth Awakening, said to be occurring in present-day America.
3. Using Diana Bass's analysis, describe the difference between the terms "religious" and "spiritual." If you were asked to choose between them, which would you select? Why?
4. Describe the events that coalesced to shape the religious discontent that emerged in the U.S. between 2000 and 2010, accounting for the period known as the "horrible decade." If you were alive at the time, were you affected by these changes? Explain your answer.
5. Explain the meaning of the author's statement, "The current problem is not just a religious problem but also a human problem."
6. What does Bass mean by the phrase "the Great Returning"? In your estimation, is the religious discontent in America today the beginning of the end for organized religion or the end of the beginning of a new global spirituality? Explain your answer.
7. What does Bass mean by the phrase "the Great Reversal"?

Chapter 12

Outgrowing Cultic Christianity

AS WE HAVE NOTICED, Christianity has changed over time, and not necessarily for the better. Philippians 2:5–8 introduces a concept called "kenosis," which means "letting go" or "self-emptying." Kenosis was the spiritual way chosen by Jesus. This path has been followed by many of the world's spiritual masters, for an obvious reason: great spirituality is about letting go. This teaching, original to many of the world's religions, has been abandoned by many modern Christians, some calling themselves "conservative," including many so-called evangelicals, and they have turned original Christianity from a concern with those in need (from solidarity with those in need) to a concern with one's own need for salvation, from losing one's self (ego) to "saving one's soul." Disavowing the notion of self-negation or self-emptying that characterized the original followers of Jesus, many modern Christians have bought into spiritual capitalism, focusing less on self-denial than on self-affirmation, which in the United States and other developed Western nations has come to be associated with materialism, consumerism, prosperity, and economic surplus. As a result of all this material acquisition, modern Christians suffer from perpetual dissatisfaction, for they never seem to have enough. There is always another gadget to buy, another necessity to increase our pleasure and ease, and our souls suffocate for lack of spiritual oxygen.

Tyranny of the Ego

In the past, there were always individuals with inflated egos—some became monarchs, dictators, or conquerors—but in the Western world today, the cultivation of the ego is seen as the ideal for everyone. Individualism permeates almost everything we do. The worship of the ego has become the cult of the West. The cultural ideal of the Western industrialized world is the self-made, self-sufficient, autonomous individual who stands solidly on both feet, not needing anyone else and not beholden to anyone for anything.

In our consumer culture, even religion and spirituality have often become a matter of addition: earning points with God, obtaining enlightenment, producing laudable moral behavior. Yet authentic spirituality is not about accumulating, attaining, achieving, performing, or even about succeeding, all of which pander to the ego. Authentic spirituality is more about letting go—of what is temporary, of what we don't actually need. As Meister Eckhart, the medieval Christian mystic, taught, "God is not found in the soul by adding anything, but by a process of subtraction" (*Sermon on Romans 8:15*).

Like so many things that we call Christianity, we find that if we scratch beneath the surface, we find less of authentic Christianity and more of local religious culture. Thankfully, some Christians today long to clarify what is essential gospel, and what is historical or sectarian accident. The great task of religion is to keep humans fully awake, alert, and conscious. Staying awake comes not from willpower but from a wholehearted surrender to the moment—as it is. If we can accept the full reality of what is right here and now, if we can be present in this mindful way, we will experience what most of us mean by God. It is largely a matter of letting go of resistance to what the present moment offers or of clinging to a past moment.

To be awake and fully conscious spiritually, we must step back from our compulsive identification with our isolated selves. This may be the most difficult "letting go" of all, for the idea of our individual "selves" is the primary illusion of our lives. Pure consciousness is never just "me," trapped inside myself. Such consciousness, rather, requires an observing of "me" from a distance, a perspective we call the Indwelling Spirit. From this missing platform, we see with eyes much larger and clearer than our own.

Most of us do not understand this awareness because we are totally identified with our passing thoughts, feelings, and compulsive patterns of perception. Maintaining a proper distance from ourselves allows us to see our radical connectedness with everything else. Such radical connectedness is the meaning of holiness—a separation, not from reality around us, but from our possessive egos. To get started spiritually, some degree of detachment is required.

Such detachment, however, does not come by attacking our ego, for that simply creates negative energy. Rather, it comes through the disciplines of meditation and contemplation, for through these practices we become less interested in protecting our self-created, temporary identity. When we stop feeding the ego, it calmly falls away, and we experience genuine grace and humility.

In contemplation, our awareness goes deep, invading our unconscious. In this way, our view of the world changes from fear to connection, because we are no longer trapped inside our fragile ego. Nor do we feel the need to defend or protect our small and vulnerable self. In meditation, we move from ego consciousness to soul awareness, from being fear-driven to being love-drawn. To experience this reality is to know the greater vitality we call God or the Great Lover. If we can allow this Creator Reality to have its way with us, we will experience a Flow that we did not create. It is the life of the Triune God interpenetrating us, producing new birth.

Knowledge is Not the Same as Wisdom

Our society encourages "fullness," but sincere spiritual seekers resist this false truth; becoming "full" with information does not add up to wisdom. Wisdom is not the gathering of more facts and information, but rather is a different way of seeing and knowing. Nothing new—no perspective, experience, or even love—can come to us when we are full of ourselves, our agendas, or our own points of view. That is why self-emptying is so critical to any expression of authentic spirituality.

What do we mean when we speak of "self-emptying" or "loss of self"? It involves (1) breaking down our cherished self-identities, that is, our wants, desires, demands, and ego struggles, but also (2) openness of being. These do not mean loss of personality or of personality traits. Self-emptying is not an absolute state we achieve, but rather the practice of letting go. And this practice of detachment, in which we experience "the fluidity of presence" that is deeper than identity, becomes the medium for the great transformation of being that results from a contemplative, open, spiritual life. In this sense, we might say that wisdom is the freedom to be present.

People who are fully present know how to see fully, rightly, and truthfully. Such presence keeps our hearts open, our minds receptive, and our bodies fully in the moment. Protecting presence is the daily task of all mature religions and of all spiritual seekers. It is this sense of presence, open and available, that allows us to experience and participate in the life of God in the world.

Wisdom is openness of being. It is ongoing receptivity to the wonder of life. Having an ability to flow with what life offers makes us receptive to divine presence. When the ego is in charge, we find ourselves resistant to correction, needing to defend ourselves when others disagree with us, or note some inconsistency in our behavior, or some flaw in our character. Emptiness—equanimity and transformation of spirit—results when we become oriented toward surrender and receptivity.

To experience such emptiness is what the Bible calls "eternal life," a reality we can experience in the present. As Catherine of Siena declared, "It is heaven all the way to heaven and hell all the way to hell." We are in heaven when we let go, when we trust and surrender to the deeper reality that is already available to us. We are in hell when we cling to our suffering and pain, when we identify with our fears and view ourselves as victims. Any chosen state of victimhood is a dead end. If your narrative is about being changed—whether by others or even by God—you are already falling into the clutches of death and destruction.

Perhaps this is why biblical scholars maintain that the center of Jesus' teaching is about forgiveness. Forgiveness is the religious word for letting go and accepting Reality for what it is. Forgiveness does not mean accepting abuse, or passing it on, but it does mean moving out of the quicksand marked by anger, fear, and blame.

Rethinking Eternal Life

A life with God is possible in the present, even though that final life in all its fullness has not yet arrived. There is a tension throughout the New Testament between "the already and the not yet." In the gospel of John, for example, passages such as 3:17–21, 31–36, and 6:47 exemplify realized eschatology, meaning that God's long-awaited eschatological transformation of reality, including judgment of evil and reward of faith, is underway in the present, initiated by Jesus' coming into the world. The very presence of Jesus in the world confronts the world with a decision, to believe or not to believe, and making that decision is the moment of judgment. If one's life is characterized by transformative belief, so that one's deeds are "done in God" (3:21), then one is saved; if one does not believe, one is already condemned. John's gospel does include traditional understandings of eschatology and the final judgment (5:28–29; 12:48), but judgment and eternal life as present realities are at the theological heart of the Fourth Gospel.

For the author of the Fourth Gospel, God's judgment of the world arises out of God's love for the world. When God sent Jesus, God presented the world with a critical moment of decision. In each person's decision whether to accept God's offer of salvation, the world judges itself. Decision and self-judgment define Johannine eschatology. In New Testament scholar Rudolf Bultmann's eloquent words, the Fourth Gospel expresses "a radical understanding of Jesus' appearance as the eschatological event. This event puts an end to the old course of the world. From now on there are only believers and unbelievers, only saved and lost, those who have life and who are in death. This is because the event is grounded in the love of God, that love which gives life to faith, but which must become judgment in the face of unbelief."[1]

"Eternal life," the term John uses instead of "kingdom of God," is not something believers possess only after death. It begins as soon as one places trust in Jesus as God's Son. Contemporary Christians have become so used to associating eternal life with going to heaven that the idea of realized eschatology, which views the future as somehow present now, seems perplexing. The notion of "eternal life," like "kingdom of God," is paradoxical at its core. Eternal life, like the kingdom of God, (a) is already present, yet not fully so. This becomes clearer when we understand that "eternal life" has as much to do with the quality and direction of life as with the length of one's existence. A better term might be "everlasting life," meaning a life that begins for believers in this lifetime but continues on forever. Eternal life (b) is a gift of God, yet it requires belief and is validated by bearing good fruit; and eternal life (c) has a spiritual nature, yet is related to physical existence. According to Pauline expectation, human existence will continue in bodily form ("further clothed"; 2 Cor 5:4) after death.

---

1. Bultmann, *John*, 159.

When Jesus is quoted in John's Gospel as saying that he has come to give others life, and give it abundantly (10:10), he was speaking of eternal life as a present reality. He was divulging his grandest teaching: The human quest for eternal life is not based on the claim that one might live after death, but rather on an awareness that self-conscious human life already shares in the eternity of God. Eternal life is experienced in the present to the degree that one is in communion with that life-enhancing power of love we call God. Meister Eckhart claimed that the highest parting for humans comes when "for God's sake we take leave of God." While we cannot be sure what Eckhart had in mind, one way to construe his enigmatic expression is to shift our image of God from one who is external to one who is internal, recognizing that we are already "in God." To embrace this recognition is to experience what the Bible calls "eternal life."

Rethinking the Kingdom of God

While the apocalyptic Jesus seems to have taught that the kingdom of God had not yet arrived, later Christians taught that it is a present reality, at least in part. How, then, should twenty-first Christians understand this teaching? Here is my take on the subject.

The kingdom of God is not something primarily political, economic, or even religious, though it does not ignore these realms. It is not about vengeance, retribution, or divine wrath. It is not something into which we die, but rather it is a reality to which we awaken. It is a metaphor for a state of consciousness, not a place to which we go, but a place from which we come. It signifies an entirely new way of looking at the world, a transformed awareness that turns our world into a different reality. This awareness sees no separation—not between God or humans, humans and other humans, body and soul, or soul and nature. This mindset is about indwelling and interrelatedness (note Jesus' metaphor of the vine and branches in John 15:4–5, 9). Only by mutual "inter-abiding" can we experience God's kingdom and fulfill God's Great Commandment—loving God and neighbor as ourselves (see Matt 20:39)—naturally and effortlessly. Stage Four in our journey of faith provides this new and complete way of seeing and understanding that your neighbor is you. There are not two individuals out there, simply temporary cells of the one great Life.

The kingdom of God is not a world without pain or mystery, but simply a world where people are connected and in communion with all things. The kingdom is about union and communion, which means it is also about mercy, forgiveness, nonviolence, letting go, solidarity, service, and simplicity, as Jesus' teachings make clear. In this reign of God, the very motive for rivalry, greed, and violence is negated, for all are part of God's Beloved Community. In other words, God's kingdom is the antithesis of Christendom, a man-made imperial system wedded to condemnation, violence, and control. The gospel flourishes only in the realm of freedom and love, not in the realm of imposition and fear.

However, the kingdom's freedom is one we must choose for ourselves, one we cannot choose unless we have glimpsed its attractive alternative to what seems like the only game in town—be it political, economic, or religious. Jesus was not intent on establishing a new religion, that is, on making the world formally Christian. Rather, his vision was based on the truth that right relatedness and the power of powerlessness would save the world from self-destruction.

If there will be a new heaven and a new earth, as the book of Revelation indicates, if God's kingdom will one day fully manifest itself on earth, as Matthew indicates, and if there will be a future resurrection, as 1 Corinthians 15 declares, then Christians must be concerned not only about heavenly things but also about earthly things—for all creation shall one day be redeemed (Rom 8:19–20). No one should be more concerned about caring for the earth and matters of global import than Christians, since our concerns are evidently God's concern as well. God not only made creation, God loves creation, and is in the process of redeeming it. It is an impoverished vision of the gospel "that cares for the souls of the unsaved but not their bodies or minds, that cares for heaven but not the conditions on earth, that cares for spiritual things but not also material things."[2]

Rethinking Faith, Belief, and Fact

When we embrace Stage Four living and thinking, we come to love ourselves more authentically, as an extension of God and others. We also love the Bible more; even old beliefs begin to shine again, but in fresh ways:[3]

1. Sin is viewed, not as a legal infraction for which we fear punishment, but as a relational disconnection, a broken solidarity, a harm inflicted upon the common good when we fail to live in love.

---

2. Witherington, *John's Wisdom*, 113.
3. This list is adapted from McLaren, *Faith After Doubt*, 156–57.

2. Salvation is viewed, not as an evacuation plan to get souls into heaven after death, but as a transformation plan to bring justice and peace for the earth and all its creatures.

3. Incarnation is viewed, not as a one-time exceptional event, but as a window into God's inter-being with all of humanity and even all of creation.

4. Jesus' death is viewed, not as a blood sacrifice necessary to lessen divine wrath, but as a revelation of self-giving love facing down systemic cruelty with death-defying nonviolence.

5. Resurrection is viewed, not as a single resuscitation alone, but as the uprising of a new humanity, filled with the ongoing embodiment of God-with-us.

6. The gospel is viewed, not as information about how to avoid hell, but as good news for all people.

7. The kingdom of God is viewed, not as a dualistic, other-worldly reality for the privileged, but as a better way to live, a better path to walk, a path of love available to all right now, just as we are.

8. Trinity is viewed, not as a math problem or test of orthodoxy, but as divine interbeing, divine relationality at the source and center of the universe.

9. The Bible is viewed, not as a law code justifying us or condemning others, but as a library containing a treasury of poetry, arguments, insights, stories, models, and more, useful to inspire and equip us in our mutual liberation today, just as our ancestors in the faith were in their day.

In Stage Four of faith, we find ourselves moving from what we believe to be true factually to something deeper and truer, namely, to what is happening actually. For example, whether or not the creation story happened factually as described in Genesis, we commit to live in the world as if it actually were a precious, beautiful, meaningful creation. Whether or not the Exodus story factually happened in history, we commit to live in the world as if all humans were actually on a journey from oppression to liberation. Whether or not Jesus was factually born of a literal virgin, or walked on literal water, or multiplied literal bread, or was raised bodily from the dead, we commit to live in the world as if what seems humanly impossible may actually become possible if we dare to live generously, against all odds.

What matters most is not that we believe the stories or their doctrinal interpretations, but that we believe in the meaning they carry so that we can act upon that meaning and embody it in our lives, letting that meaning animate and fill us. To our surprise, when we receive permission to doubt the factuality of our beliefs, we discover their actual life-giving purpose. Faith and doubt together make us who we are. We cannot live without either.

Questions for Discussion and Reflection

1. Define and assess the meaning of the term "spiritual capitalism." Does this concept adequately describe the current religious ethos in America?

2. In the author's estimation, is there an antidote to spiritual capitalism? If so, what is it?

3. What is meant by the phrase "tyranny of the ego"? How does this tyranny manifest itself in your life? In your experience, is detachment from one's possessive ego advisable or even possible? Explain your answer.

4. Biblical scholars indicate that where the synoptic authors speak of the kingdom of God, the gospel of John substitutes the phrase "eternal life." In your estimation, are these expressions synonymous? If so, to what extent was Jesus' term "kingdom of God" fluid during the first century, fluctuating from an original apocalyptic meaning to a non-apocalyptic meaning?

5. In your estimation, what does it mean to live like a "kingdom person" in American society today?

6. After completing this book (or class or seminar), what is the primary insight you received? (If possible, state it in one sentence.) Has this book changed your religious claims or beliefs? Has it changed your behavior or your priorities? Has it changed the way you relate to God, to yourself, and to others? If so, how?

7. After completing this book, have you encountered any elements of the apocalyptic mindset in your own thinking you need to reaffirm?

Have you encountered any elements of apocalyptic thinking you need to relinquish?

8. After completing this book, what have you learned about "living into a new way of thinking"?
9. After completing this book, what message do you bring for our society and planet?

Appendix A

The Unfolding Drama of Faith in the Biblical Storyline

PEOPLE TRAPPED IN CULTIC mindsets or authoritarian faith systems cannot grow spiritually without intervention. Intervention can be external—that is, through deprogramming, persuasion, intercession, or mediation by parents, friends, caregivers, or clergy—or internal—that is, coming to one's senses, whether by experiencing disappointment, parting ways with cultic mentors and friends, or simply by moving on from one phase of faith or belief to another.

When persons become aware that they are in a cultic group or under the influence of an authoritarian leader, they must act on that awareness immediately, questioning the movement and its leaders, including friends still committed to the group or under its influence. They must act on their doubts and questions, in some cases forsaking the movement in order to allow themselves to grow and change spiritually.

While the Bible can be read for theological information, it also provides a narrative in faith formation, for all four stages of faith appear in the biblical storyline. The biblical narrative begins with Torah, that is, with teaching suitable to Stage One formative faith, including stories of beginnings, both of the cosmos and of the Hebrew people as a theocratic community in covenant relationship with God. It then moves into the monarchical or kingdom phase, where the covenant community becomes unified as Israel before dividing into two kingdoms, northern Israel and southern Judah. Over time, both kingdoms come to an end politically, in the exilic and postexilic phases. For Christians, the biblical narrative does not end with postexilic Judaism, but rather moves through the Intertestamental Period to its culmination in Jesus, the apostolic period, and the emergence of the church.

In general ways, this division parallels the approach of the noted Old Testament scholar Bernhard Anderson in his *The Unfolding Drama of the Bible*. In that work, Anderson follows a dramatic pattern of three acts, building on three crucial events in the biblical drama (1) the exodus from Egypt and the path to nationhood; (2) the exile into Babylon and the return to the homeland; and (3) the crucifixion and resurrection of Jesus, which in the church age reconstitutes the people of God into a global movement.

Our approach differs from Anderson's in two critical ways. First, our discussion examines the biblical narratives, not as "mighty acts" or events, as Anderson proposes, but as long historical processes composed of turns, surprises, and alternatives. The recital of these histories is not a neat scheme, but rather a slow torturous process. Second, these events or histories are not three in number but four, corresponding with the overlapping phases of faith development introduced in chapters 3 and 6 above and labeled as Stages One through Four or more succinctly as Simplicity, Complexity, Perplexity, and Clarity (Harmony).

Stage One (Simplicity). In terms of the life of faith, we begin with the stories of Israel's ancestors found in Genesis 12–50.[1] Israel is embodied in Abraham, Isaac, and Jacob (and their wives and progeny), sojourners on their way to nationhood and community, bound in responses to the call of God who tells them little of himself and asks of them a blind trust. They are Stage One people. They are the people of sojourn, a term often described as "resident alien"; in English, the "sojourn" is commonly called "pilgrimage." To observers, the pilgrims are simply coping and surviving like all other human beings. Insiders know they are not simply coping, but rather that they are on their way toward a promise of place and belonging, a realization that greatly changes the nature of the sojourn.

In this opening phase of faith, guided by legislation, authority, and above all by covenant relationship with God, the people of faith are characterized by hope and anticipation of security and prosperity in a place of promise—a Promised Land. Finally, after forty years of wandering in the wilderness, the exodus period is completed and Israel comes to the land of promise. The crossing of the Jordan marks a decisive boundary in the

---

1. The discussion that follows is inspired by Brueggemann's text, *The Land*. In our adaptation, we borrow his thesis and language while changing the focus.

history of faith. Entry into the Promised Land, beginning with conquest and settlement, drastically redefines who the people will be.

Stage Two (Complexity). At the Jordan, the people hesitate, a pause dramatically captured in the book of Deuteronomy. With good reason, at that moment Israel pauses to do what it does when it is most characteristically Israel—it listens. In that speaking/hearing moment, when Moses speaks and Israel listens, a new Israel is called into being, one appropriate for the new time, for the next phase in its faith development. It is as though Israel's traditionalists had known intuitively that Stage Two Complexity was the time of destiny, as though Israel knew that hard, disciplined reflection is never more needed than at this moment, when the new situation of rootedness requires a new Israel with a new faith.

The long pause of Deuteronomy is presented as though Israel is reluctant to put its feet in the Jordan, dry though it would be, because it knows that in so doing, it is leaving behind the securities of Stage One Simplicity. In this phase, in contrast to Stage One, there are no rocks to strike for water, no manna to be received for daily food. Perhaps Israel's hesitation is not from fear of leaving initial faith behind, but in the face of an ominous recognition that adulthood means life must deepen and faith must be redefined.

God's faithful people at all times linger at this transition to reflect as did Israel, because that moment stands as a paradigm for what is under way at the boundary of the new land, fraught with problems and loaded with promise. As we cross our Jordans, identity questions must all be addressed anew.

The rhetoric at the boundary is that of pure gift, of radical grace (Deut 6:10–11). There is no hint of achievement or merit or even of planning. In a peculiar way, Stage Two is much like Stage One: unplanned by Israel, it wells up with life-giving power, in inscrutable ways. Like Stage One, Stage Two faith is all promise (Josh 21:45; 23:14), filled with hope and security (Deut 8:7–10). Unlike Stage One faith, water need not come at the last moment, incredibly from a rock. Its sources are visible and reliable. Spiritual food does not need to appear surprisingly; it rises up from the land of promise as gift. Such terrain makes possible the living of a less vulnerable life, the kind it had yearned for in youth and in sojourn. Israel after Jordan is less exposed, more guaranteed. Like Israel, many Christians choose to remain in Stage Two faith, for despite its Complexity, it is fulfilling and secure (see Deut 11:10–12).

However, Stage Two faith provides secured people with dangerous temptations. Being rooted and grounded in faith invites people of faith to individuality, to enter life apart from covenant and community, to reduce covenant demands and possibilities to serene space without demand or mystery. Stage Two faith can lead to self-sufficiency, to comfortable security and complacency, changing focus from compassion and security to purity and identity, to love of God apart from love of neighbor.

In Stage Two, living with guaranteed security makes one susceptible to idolatry, including materialism, power and privilege, and even to subtle or overt racism, sexism, and other forms of supremacy. It can also make one susceptible to disinformation, conspiracy theories, cultic sectarianism, and self-serving forms of worship, Bible-reading, and theology. With its new security, Stage Two faith is susceptible to nonhistorical mindsets, including apocalyptic and dualistic flights of fantasy.

In Israel's case, Stage Two faith led to kingship, a form of leadership intended to secure and protect covenant priorities. However, this theory of government led to a loss of covenantal history. In practically every instance, royal theology led to corruption. To counter royal privilege and abuse of power, prophets arose precisely to address kings, calling them to accountability. An obvious example is that of Ahab and Elijah in 1 Kings 21, though we must not forget royal abuse under the best of kings, such as Nathan's rebuke of King David in 2 Samuel 11–12. To his credit, David repented, that is, he responded to the prophetic rebuke with a total reorientation of being, something nearly impossible for people in situations of supremacy and in positions of authority (see Jer 13:23).

David's ambivalence is gone in his son Solomon. Here is a king totally secure in his land, totally committed to keeping his turf on his own terms while insensitive to the cry of his subjects or to the claims of God. In 1 Kings 11:29–39, the prophet Ahijah warns of coming judgment: the land will be lost, the kingdom will be revoked, and the glory of Jerusalem will be diminished. To be sure, the dynasty will survive for a time, but only temporarily, and in reduced form. The same can be said for any kingdom or rule of the future, be it political, economic, or religious in nature. In Israel, royal history moved inexorably toward exile.

God's course of action against religious and political supremacy is best presented by Jeremiah, who describes presumptuous complacency and power in 22:13: "Woe to him who builds his house by unrighteousness, and his upper rooms by injustice." "Is not this to know me?" says the Lord in Jeremiah 22:16, placing the cause of the poor and needy above merit and gain, a standard reiterated in the New Testament (see Jas 1:27). Thus Jeremiah, most powerful of Israel's prophets, announces to Israel that its time in the Promised Land is over (see Jer 21:1–14; 23:1–40).

Stage Three (Perplexity). The Babylonian exile is the great watershed in the history of Israelite religion, for it marks an ending but also a beginning; the life of the people of Israel ends, but the history of Judaism begins.

Having delivered the bad news ("to pluck up and to pull down, to destroy and to overthrow"), Jeremiah then returns to the second part of his message, "to build and to plant" (1:10). Jeremiah's message is not simply judgment to those secure in Stage Two forms of faith. It offers promise to the exiles in Stage Three, for as it turns out, exile (loss of land, guarantees, privilege, and security) is the way to Stage Four faith (return to the new land). Exile is the way to new life in a new land. One can scarcely imagine a less likely understanding of faith: uncertainty is the root to certainty; unknowing is the way to knowing; in New Testament categories, embracing death is the way to life (Luke 9:23–27).

Jeremiah announces the central scandal of the Bible, that radical loss and discontinuity are the source of real newness, that the exiles are the true heirs (Jer 24:4–7). Conversely, those who cling to the land (to privilege and the status quo) are exiled from God (24:8–10). Outsiders and the disinherited, whom the privileged world does not value, are the ones who belong; those who remain in the land (Stage Two) are the dispossessed. In covenant terms, the cursed are blessed, and the blessed are cursed.

We find this message of inversion again in the Beatitudes (see Matt 5:3–12; Luke 6:20–26). Jesus' understanding of faith, of power and powerlessness, of gain and loss, is not the reading done by kings and empires, by legislators and captains of industry, or by popes and bishops, but by this strange God who always provides an alternative reading of faith and truth, of gain and loss, of sin and salvation.

In this respect, there is no more radical text than the parable of figs in Jeremiah 24, for it is the God of Israel who announces exile as the way of the future. Newness comes in discontinuity and loss. It is among exiles that God calls into existence things that do not exist (Rom 4:17). That is the message of the New Testament; that is the message of crucifixion and the power of resurrection, that God reduces to nothing things that are (1 Cor 1:28), that the one "despised and rejected by others" (Isa 53:3) is the heir to the future. In Israel's epic exilic struggle are the seeds of crucifixion/resurrection faith. Landed or not, privileged or not, religiously secure or not, people of faith are pressed to radical reliance on the God who works newness precisely where it can't seem to be—in exile.[2]

History can end; it does end. But the One who tears down, builds up; the One who plucks up, plants; the One who reduces to nothing things that are is the One who can call into existence things that do not exist. And that is the extraordinary thing in the Bible; the Lord of history gives history to those who have no history. This God makes the barren mothers of promise, the slaves bearers of freedom, the hungry heirs of the promise, and hopeless exiles God's new people.

That is the word from the Lord to Stage Three people. Where one's history has ended, history begins anew—not continued, but begun anew. And God's word is precisely to exiles: "Build houses and live in them; plant gardens and eat what they produce. Take wives and have sons and daughters.... But seek the welfare of the city where I have sent you into exile, and pray to the Lord on its behalf, for in its welfare you will find your welfare. For thus says the Lord of hosts, the God of Israel: Do not let the prophets and the diviners who are among you deceive you, and do not listen to the dreams that they dream, for it is a lie that they are prophesying to you in my name; I did not send them, says the Lord.... For surely I know the plans I have for you, says the Lord, plans for your welfare and not for harm, to give you a future with hope" (Jer 29:5-11). This is the new covenant of which Jeremiah speaks in 31:31-34, and of which the New Testament speaks as having been mediated by Jesus (see Heb 8:6-12).

Among the exilic prophets, another remarkable attempt to anticipate the fourth new history is Ezekiel. His tradition is most radical in that it announces both the end of Stages One and Two faith history and yet the longing of Stage Four faith in most decisive terms. In chapters 4-5 Ezekiel dramatizes the end, an end he declares in chapter 7. In 9:9 the prophet adds an unexpected image, the Lord's departure from Judah and Jerusalem. The damage being done by Israel's organized religion (see Amos 5:21-24) is not only to the land and the people but also to God, who does not simply choose to leave, but is forced out by intolerable injustice and vacuity, in business and in worship.

Ezekiel's imagery is more extreme than Jeremiah's. In Jeremiah, the prophet and the Lord grieve over Israel's exile. In Ezekiel, the Lord

---

2. Calling himself a "believer in exile," meaning a believer who increasingly lives at odds with the ways in which Christianity has traditionally been proclaimed, bishop John Shelby Spong addresses his 1998 bestselling book, *Why Christianity Must Change or Die* to fellow religious exiles, using the subtitle "A Bishop Speaks to Believers in Exile."

himself is in exile; God is in exile, along with other exiles, in Babylon. Not only is history over for Israel; it has ended for the Lord as well. In the New Testament, we find this image again with Jesus on the cross, in the presence of an exiled God. In the Bible, the exile is not only a decisive turn for the people of Israel; it is also a decisive turn in the history of God. In the Old Testament, the temple, the locus of organized worship, is destroyed, as it will be again a generation after Jesus' death. In exile, not only do people of faith begin anew; in exile, God also begins history anew. In exile, God's sovereignty is present in a double capacity: as one who ends history, but also as one who initiates history. In initiating history, God recreates humanity, bringing life out of death.

It is in the context of exile that Israel tells its best stories, including the creation story found in Genesis 1:1–2:4a. From this new setting we can reexamine this old account, understanding clearly and perhaps for the first time the meaning and purpose of chaos language ("formless void," *tohu wahobu*) in Genesis 1:2 as a reference not to the original act of creation, but rather to exile as chaos. Read historically and contextually, the text contrasts Israel's future (Stage Four faith) with Israel's exilic present (Stage Three faith), surely the experience of the faithful in Babylon.

A central theme of Israel's stories for exiles is that to the barren is born the child of promise, for those without promise or hope are given the impossible blessing (Gen 11:30; 18:9–15; 25:21; 29:31). Israel's stories now shaped into final form are not about barrenness, but about inviting exiles to reconsider their destiny. In the exile, Israel told stories of rootage, belonging, and promise.

Stage Four (Clarity). According to Ezekiel, God performs a total-body makeover, or rather, a "faith transplant": "A new heart I will give you, and a new spirit I will put within you; and I will remove from your body the heart of stone and give you a heart of flesh. I will put my spirit within you . . . and you shall be my people, and I will be your God" (36:26–28). If a new history now begins, it must be rooted in God and not in Israel or in any traditional religious leaders. No longer will Israel's priests shepherd the flock, for in serving their own needs rather than the flock's, Israel's traditional worship leaders have abdicated their role. Now it is not traditional clergy to whom God's flock must turn for guidance and sustenance: "Thus says the Lord God, I am against the shepherds . . . ; no longer shall the shepherds feed themselves. I will rescue my sheep from their mouths, so that they may not be food for them" (34:10).

In chapter 37, Ezekiel again speaks of the end of exile and of return to the land, this time in the bold imagery of resurrection: "Thus says the Lord God: I am going to open your graves, and bring you up from your graves, O my people; and I will bring you back to the land of Israel" (37:12). Thus, Ezekiel's speech envisions history beyond exile. First, the Lord's exile is ended. The glory that had departed to Babylon now returns to Jerusalem. However, God's promise is now expanded to include the alien and the stranger (47:21–23), an inclusivity that poses deep problems for traditionalists.

In the exile, a prophet we call Second Isaiah (Isa 40–55) announces that Israel is "comforted" (40:1; 51:3, 12, 19; 52:9; 54:11). It is Second Isaiah more than the other exilic prophets who announces a turn in history. Whatever else Second Isaiah's poetry means in terms of mission to the Gentiles and vicarious suffering, the baseline is the return home of God's exiled people. History is inverted, nature transformed. Babylonian tyranny yields to Persian liberation (45:1–7); dry places in the wilderness are transformed into nourishment (41:17–19).

Return from exile signifies a new beginning, for Israel (now called Judaism), and for Gentiles (now called to be God's people). This newness comes neither from Israel's faith nor from Persian generosity. Rather, it comes from God's will. That is the new history. In this respect, Second Isaiah makes a connection that will be important to the New Testament and to all exiles: God wills homecoming. In Stage Four faith, outcasts are comforted and given inheritance. To be comforted is to belong.

In Israel's postexilic period, the exiles respond in various ways. The purists return with vivid memory and an urgent mission. Conservative, separatist, and exclusivist, they are driven by law and order. Others remain in Babylon, faithful in their diaspora. Still others blend in, giving up their distinctives and embracing the prevailing Hellenistic culture. Yet others look forward with renewed faith and vigor to a future uncertain yet full of promise, searching for God, even groping for him . . . and finding him, for "indeed he is not far from each one of us" (Acts 17:27).

Some become sectarian, embracing apocalyptic views, longing for divine vengeance upon their enemies. Of this group, some become Christians, accepting Jesus as Messiah and believing in his alternative vision for a peaceful kingdom, based upon forgiveness and reversal, where the weak are strong and the last are first. Eventually, Jesus' death and resurrection serve as the paradigm for a new start, a universal covenant between God and all humanity, in which the meek inherit the earth.

Appendix B

The Meaning of the Millennium: Four Views[1]

THE CONCEPT OF THE millennium can be examined under four categories: (1) historic premillennialism, (2) dispensational premillennialism, (3) postmillennialism, and (4) amillennialism. (To these a fifth can be added—panmillennialism—which affirms that everything will "pan out" in the end.) Each of these interpretations involves difficulties, but the central truth of all four is the affirmation that Christ will return to destroy the forces of evil and establish God's eternal kingdom.[2]

1. *Historic premillennialism*: this view, a moderate form of premillennialism, maintains that Christ will return to earth before the millennium. Despite attempts to Christianize society, conditions will become worse as history unfolds, and in the final days the antichrist will gain control of human affairs. At Christ's return, the Christian dead will be raised and believers will reign with Christ during the millennium, the golden age of one thousand years of peace on earth. Then Satan will be released for a short period, after which all other dead will be raised. This explanation accounts for the two resurrections in Revelation 20:4-6. Finally there comes the judgment before the great white throne.

2. *Dispensational premillennialism*: this view, an extreme form of premillennialism, maintains that the purposes of God in scripture can be understood through a series of time periods called dispensations.

---

1. The material in the appendix is taken from my book, *Hope Revealed*, 194-97.

2. For a discussion of the pros and cons of each of the main views of the millennium, see Clouse, *Meaning of the Millennium*, and Grenz, *Millennial Maze*.

The basic premise of dispensationalism is the distinction between Israel and the church. Dispensationalists argue that the purposes of God are expressed in the formation of two groups, Jews and Christians, whose distinction continues throughout eternity. Exponents of this view follow a literal system of biblical interpretation, adhering to a timetable that considers everything after Revelation 4:1 as future. Since dispensationalists expect Old Testament promises to be fulfilled literally, the Jews must establish a theocratic kingdom in the land of Palestine, which they will possess forever. These predictions will be fulfilled in the millennium, a literal thousand-year period on earth.

Dispensationalists maintain that the coming of Christ before the millennium consists of two stages: the first, a secret rapture that removes living Christians from earth to meet Christ in the air (1 Thess 4:17), whence they will proceed to heaven to be spared the devastation of the Great Tribulation, a time of earthly persecution championed by the antichrist. The second stage involves Christ's coming with his saints (a select group of followers, including resurrected believers) to establish the kingdom on earth. This millennial reign, rather than being established through the conversion of individuals over a long period of time, will come about suddenly. The Jews will be converted during the millennium and will have a central role during this time. Evil will be held in check (for Satan is bound) and nature will flourish during this golden age, to the point where even ferocious beasts are tame (cf. Isa 65:25). At the end of the millennium, Satan will be released and precipitate a rebellion. Following the millennium, the non-Christian dead are raised and the eternal states of heaven and hell are established.

3. *Postmillennialism*: adherents of this view believe that Christ will come after the millennium has taken place. The kingdom of God is present on earth during the church age and is now being extended in the world through the preaching of the gospel and the saving work of the Holy Spirit. This activity is causing the world to be Christianized and will result in a lengthy period of peace and prosperity called the millennium. Christ is presently reigning through his faithful church and will bring to the world a thousand years of peace and righteousness prior to his return at the conclusion of history. According to this scenario, evil is not eliminated from history but is being minimized as the moral and spiritual influence of Christians deepens in society. As the church develops through history, it will assume such great importance that many social, economic,

and political problems will be solved. This period closes with the Second Coming of Christ, the resurrection of the dead, and the final judgment.

4. *Amillennialism*: proponents of this view regard the thousand years, like other numerals in Revelation, to be symbolic. Instead of being a literal period of exactly one thousand years, the expression refers to a long time, extending from the first to the Second Coming of Christ. During the entire period Satan is "bound," meaning that evil's power is limited by the preaching of the gospel (Luke 10:18). The "last days" correspond to the church age, a period beginning with Jesus and with the outpouring of the Holy Spirit on the day of Pentecost and ending when the "last day" arrives. Instead of the optimism of postmillennialism or the pessimism of premillennialism, amillennialists take seriously the teaching of Jesus that good and evil will develop side by side until the end of the world (Matt 13:24–30, 36–43). Amillennialists look forward to a glorious and perfect kingdom on the new earth in the life to come. Some amillennialists interpret the millennium mentioned in Revelation 20:4–6 as describing the present reign of the souls of deceased believers with Christ in heaven.

Although these interpretations are represented throughout the history of the church, in certain ages a particular outlook has dominated. During the first three centuries of the Christian era, premillennialism appears to have been the dominant eschatological interpretation. Among its adherents were Papias, Irenaeus, Justin Martyr, Tertullian, Hippolytus, Methodius, Commodianus, and Lactantius. During the fourth century, when the Christian church was given a favored status, the amillennial position was accepted. The famous church father Augustine articulated this position, which became the dominant interpretation in medieval times. His teaching was so fully accepted that at the Council of Ephesus in 421, belief in a literal millennium was condemned as superstitious. The Protestant Reformers stayed with Augustinian amillennialism, particularly in opposition to the premillennial views of Radical Reformers (Anabaptists) such as Jan Matthys, who called for the establishment of a millennial kingdom in the city of Münster, considered to be the New Jerusalem. As premillennialism waned, postmillennialism became the prevailing eschatological interpretation, receiving its most impressive formulation through the work of Daniel Whitby (1638–1726).

During the nineteenth century premillennialism again attracted widespread attention, fostered in part by the violent social and political upheaval during that period. There was also a renewed interest in the conversion and status of the Jews. The writings of J. N. Darby (1800–1882), popularized in the United States by D. L. Moody and C. I. Scofield, contributed greatly to the emergence and propagation of dispensational premillennialism. During the second half of the twentieth and the start of the twenty-first centuries, books by Hal Lindsey (particularly the bestseller titled *Late Great Planet Earth*, 1970) and the *Left Behind* series (sixteen novels written by Tim LaHaye and Jerry B. Jenkins between 1995 and 2007) greatly enhanced the popularity of dispensational premillennialism, particularly among conservative Christian audiences.

Bibliography

Alito, Frank. "36 of the most popular conspiracy theories in the U.S." No pages. Online: https://www.insider.com/ popular-conspiracy-theories-united-states-2019-5.
Allison Jr., Dale C. *Constructing Jesus*. Grand Rapids, MI: Baker, 2010.
———. *The Historical Christ and the Theological Jesus*. Grand Rapids, MI: Eerdmans, 2009.
———. *Jesus of Nazareth: Millenarian Prophet*. Minneapolis, MN: Fortress, 1998.
Anderson, Bernhard W. *The Unfolding Drama of the Bible*. 4th ed. Minneapolis: Fortress, 1988.
Armstrong, Karen. *The Case for God*. New York: Anchor, 2010.
———. *A Short History of Myth*. New York: Canongate, 2005.
Bass, Diana Butler. *Christianity After Religion; The End of Church and the Birth of a New Spiritual Awakening*. New York: HarperOne, 2012.
Borg, Marcus J. *The God We Never Knew*. New York: HarperSanFrancisco, 1998.
———. *The Heart of Christianity: Rediscovering a Life of Faith*. New York: Harper SanFrancisco, 2003.
———. *Meeting Jesus Again for the First Time*. New York: HarperSanFrancisco, 1995.
———. *Reading the Bible Again for the First Time*. New York: HarperSanFrancisco, 2002.
Borg, Marcus, and N. T. Wright. *The Meaning of Jesus: Two Visions*. New York: HarperSanFrancisco, 2000.
Boring, M. Eugene. *Revelation*. Interpretation: A Bible Commentary for Teaching and Preaching. Louisville: John Knox, 1989.
Bowes, Shauna M., and Scott O. Lilienfeld. "Looking Under the Tinfoil Hat: Clarifying the Psychological and Psychopathological Correlates of Conspiracy Beliefs." *Journal of Personality* (August 27, 2020). No pages. Online: https//doi.org/10.1111/jopy.12588.
Bradley, Marion Zimmer. *The Mists of Avalon*. New York, Knopf, 1982.
Brueggemann, Walter. *The Land*. Philadelphia: Fortress, 1977.
Bultmann, Rudolf. *The Gospel of John: A Commentary*. Translated by G. R. Beasley-Murray, R. W. N. Hoare, and J. K. Riches. Philadelphia: Westminster, 1971.
Carey, Benedict. "A Theory About Conspiracy Theories." *New York Times* (September 28, 2020). No pages. Online: https://www.nytimes.com/2020/09/28/health/psychology-conspiracy-theories.html.
Clouse, Robert H. *The Meaning of the Millennium*. Downers Grove, IL: InterVarsity, 1977.

Cox, Daniel A., and John Halpin. "Conspiracy theories, misinformation, COVID-19, and the 2020 election." No pages. Online: https://www.aei.org/research-products/report/conspiracy-theories-misinformation-covid-19-and-the-2020-election/.

Crossan, John Dominic. *Jesus: A Revolutionary Biography*. San Francisco: Harper SanFrancisco, 1994.

Crossan, John Dominic, and Richard G. Watts. *Who is Jesus?* Louisville, KY: Westminster John Knox, 1996.

Ehrman, Bart D. *A Brief Introduction to the New Testament*. 3rd ed. New York: Oxford University Press, 2013.

———. *The Historical Jesus. Course Guidebook*. Chantilly, VA: The Great Courses, 2000.

———. *Jesus: Apocalyptic Prophet of the New Millennium*. New York: Oxford University Press, 1999.

———. *The New Testament: A Historical Introduction to the Early Christian Writings*. 7th ed. New York: Oxford University Press, 2020.

———. *The New Testament. Course Guidebook*. Chantilly, Virginia: Teaching Company, 2000.

Esposito, John, et al. *World Religions Today*. New York: Oxford University Press, 2001.

Fowler, James. *Stages of Faith: The Psychology of Human Development and the Quest for Meaning*. San Francisco: HarperSanFrancisco, 1995.

Frum, David. *Trumpocalypse: Restoring American Democracy*. New York: HarperCollins, 2020.

Grenz, Stanley J. *The Millennial Maze: Sorting out Evangelical Options*. Downers Grove, IL: InterVarsity, 1992.

Griffin, David Ray. *Reenchantment without Supernaturalism: A Process Philosophy of Religion*. Ithaca, NY: Cornell University Press, 2001.

Hamilton, William. *The New Essence of Christianity*. New York: Association, 1966.

Haught, John F. *Deeper Than Darwin: The Prospect for Religion in the Age of Evolution*. Boulder, CO: Westview, 2003.

———. *God After Darwin: A Theology of Evolution*. Boulder, CO: Westview, 2000.

———. *The Promise of Nature: Ecology and Cosmic Purpose*. Mahwah, NJ: Paulist, 1993.

———. *Responses to 101 Questions on God and Evolution*. Mahwah, NJ: Paulist, 2001.

———. *Science and Religion: From Conflict to Conversation*. Mahwah, NJ: Paulist, 1995.

———. *What is God? How to Think About the Divine*. Mahwah, NJ: Paulist, 1986.

Hoekema, Anthony A. *The Four Major Cults*. Grand Rapids, MI: Eerdmans, 1963.

Hunt, David. *Cult Explosion*. Eugene, OR: Harvest House, 1980.

Jones, Robert P. *White Too Long: The Legacy of White Supremacy in American Christianity*. New York: Simon & Schuster, 2020.

Keating, Christopher. "Quinnipiac Poll." *Hartford Courant* (December 10, 2020). No pages. Online: https:// www. courant.com/politics/hc-pol-q-poll-republicans-believe-fraud-20201210-pcie3uqqvrhyvnt7geohhsyepe-story.html.

Knox, John. *The Humanity and Divinity of Christ*. Cambridge: Cambridge University Press. 1967.

Kreeft, Peter. *Three Philosophies of Life*. San Francisco: Ignatius, 1990.

Kuhn, Thomas, *The Structure of Scientific Revolutions*. 4th edition. Chicago: Chicago University Press, 2012.

Küng, Hans. *Does God Exist?* Translated by Edward Quinn. New York: Doubleday, 1980.

Lewis, C. S. *The Abolition of Man*. New York: Macmillan, 1947.

Bibliography

Loftus, John W. *The Christian Delusion: Why Faith Fails*. Amherst, NY: Prometheus, 2010.
Mackintosh, H. R. *The Doctrine of the Person of Jesus Christ*. Edinburgh: T. & T. Clark, 1913.
Martin, Walter. *The Kingdom of the Cults*. Rev. ed. Minneapolis, MN: Bethany, 2003.
———. *The New Cults*. Santa Ana, CA: Vision House, 1980.
McLaren, Brian. *Everything Must Change: Jesus, Global Crises, and a Revolution of Hope*. Nashville: Thomas Nelson, 2007.
———. *Faith After Doubt: Why Your Beliefs Stopped Working and What to Do About It*. New York: St. Martin's, 2021.
———. *A Generous Orthodoxy*. Grand Rapids, MI: Zondervan, 2004.
———. *Naked Spirituality: A Life with God in 12 Simple Words*. New York: HarperOne, 2011.
McLaren, Brian, and Gareth Higgins. *The Seventh Story: Us, Them, and the End of Violence*. Cleveland, TN: Porch, 2018
Michener, James. *The Source*. New York: Random House, 1965.
Moltmann, Jürgen. *God in Creation: A New Theology of Creation and the Spirit of God*. Minneapolis, MN: Fortress, 1993.
Naftulin, Julia. "People are more likely to believe conspiracy theories if they are anxious, detached, or narcissistic, researchers find." *Insider* (October 1, 2020). No pages. Online: https://www.insider.com/people-believe-conspiracy-theories-if-they-are-detached-narcissistic-2020-10.
Newberg, Andrew. *The Spiritual Brain: Science and Religious Experience*. Course Guidebook. Chantilly, VA: The Great Courses, 2012.
Pramuk, Christopher. *At Play in Creation: Merton's Awakening to the Feminine Divine*. Collegeville, MN: Liturgical, 2015.
Richardson, Alan. *Genesis I–XI*. Torch Commentary. London: SCM, 1953.
Rohr, Richard. *Falling Upward: A Spirituality for the Two Halves of Life*. San Francisco: Jossey-Bass, 2011.
———. *Immortal Diamond: The Search for Our True Self*. San Francisco: Jossey-Bass, 2013.
———. *The Naked Now: Learning to See as the Mystics See*. New York: Crossroad, 2009.
———. *The Universal Christ*. New York: Convergent, 2019.
———. *What the Mystics Know*. New York: Crossroad, 2015.
Sanders, E. P. *Jesus and Judaism*. Philadelphia: Fortress, 1985.
———. "Jesus: His Religious Type," *Reflections* 87 (1992) 4–12.
Schulweis, Harold M. *For Those Who Can't Believe*. New York: Harper Perennial, 1995.
Schweitzer, Albert. *The Quest of the Historical Jesus*. New York: Macmillan, 1968.
Shapiro, Rami. *Perennial Wisdom for the Spiritually Independent*. Woodstock, VT: Skylight Independent, 2013.
Smith, Huston. *Forgotten Truth: The Common Vision of the World's Religions*. New York: HarperSanFrancisco, 1976.
Spong, John Shelby. *Eternal Life: A New Vision*. New York: HarperOne, 2009.
———. *Why Christianity Must Change or Die: A Bishop Speaks to Believers in Exile*. New York: HarperOne, 1999.
Tucker, Ruth A. *Another Gospel: Cults, Alternative Religions, and the New Age Movement*. Grand Rapids, MI: Zondervan, 1989.

Vande Kappelle. Robert P. *Hope Revealed: The Message of the Book of Revelation–Then and Now*. Eugene: OR: Wipf & Stock, 2013.

———. *Refined by Fire: Essential Teachings in Scripture*. Eugene, OR: Wipf & Stock, 2018.

———. *Securing Life: The Enduring Message of the Bible*. Eugene, OR: Wipf & Stock, 2016.

———. *Wisdom Revealed: The Message of Biblical Wisdom Literature–Then and Now*. Eugene, OR: Wipf & Stock, 2014

Weber, Eugen, *Apocalypses: Prophecies, Cults, and Millennial Beliefs through the Ages*. Cambridge, MA: Harvard University Press, 1999.

Whitehead, Alfred North. *Process and Reality*. Rev. ed. New York: Free Press, 1978.

———. *Science and the Modern World*. New York: Free Press, 1967.

Witherington III, Ben. *John's Wisdom: A Commentary on the Fourth Gospel*. Louisville: Westminster John Knox, 1995.

Index

afterlife, belief in, viii, 53, 67, 68, 126
Allison, Dale, 111
amillennialism, 163, 165
apocalypses, 106
apocalyptic/ism, 104–34
   definition of, 130
   See also "last-day/end-time" thinking
apophatic, 59n17
Aquinas, Thomas, 40, 52
Armstrong, Karen, 133
Augustine of Hippo, 36, 40, 51, 66, 84, 93, 165
authority, authoritarian, ix, 13, 21, 22, 24, 25, 26, 27, 29
Awakenings in American history, 136–42

Barth, Karl, 52
Bass, Diana, 139, 140, 141, 142, 143
beliefs, religious, 9, 10, 20, 27, 28, 39, 42, 48, 95, 143, 151–53
Bible, 51, 61–78, 151, 152
   core teachings, 66–67, 73–75
   and faith development, 155–62
   inerrancy of, 62
   interpretation of, 63–64, 95
   sacredness of, 61–62, 69
   storyline of, viii, 66, 91
Biden, Joseph, 3, 4, 7, 8
Bonhoeffer, Dietrich, 58
Book of Mormon, the, 18–19
Borg, Marcus, 39n4, 56, 57, 111
Bowes, Shauna, 6, 7
Bradley, Marion Zimmer, 51
Brooks, Phillips, 93

Buber, Martin, 51, 91
Bultmann, Rudolph, 149
Burns, Ken, 130
Bush, George W., 141

Campbell, Joseph, viii, 36
Carey, Benedict, 6
Catherine of Siena, 148
Christ Archetype, viii
conspiracy theories, 1–10
   definition of, 1
contextual credibility, criterion of, 114–15, 116
COVID-19 pandemic, 3, 6, 130
Cox, Harvey, 137, 138
creation, doctrine of, viii, 80–88
cultism, 12–19, 25, 31, 72
   definition of, 15, 72
   mindset, ix, 13–14
   outgrowing, 145–53
   personalities, ix, 5, 6–7, 13–17, 21, 131

Darby, J. N., 166
Day of the Lord, 106, 108–9
dispensationalism, 105, 163–64, 166
dissimilarity, criterion of, 113–14, 116, 117
Dostoyevsky, Fyodor, 29
doubt, 22, 23, 24, 25, 26, 27, 38, 39, 45, 78, 153
dualism, viii, ix, 24, 25, 27, 28, 33–34, 50, 75, 89, 94, 106, 109, 152
   complementary, 90
   conflict, 90

Ecclesiastes, book of, 75–78, 84, 85
Eckhart, Meister, 146, 150
Eddy, Mary Baker, 136
Ehrman, Bart, 106
Eliade, Mircea, 34
Eliot, T. S., 28
Erikson, Erik, 21
eschatology, 85, 108, 110–12, 122–27
    apocalyptic, 125
    inaugurated, 128, 130, 131
    prophetic, 125
    realized, 129, 131, 148–49
Esposito, John, 34, 35
eternal life, 105, 106, 116, 131, 148–50

faith, 143, 152, 153
    and the Bible, 71–73
    definition of, 39–43, 50
    and the human brain, 43–45
    transformative, 83
faith formation, 15, 21–31, 72, 75, 132, 150
Fowler, James, 6, 21, 22
framing story, vii
Freemasonry, 2

God, viii, 97
    belief in, 47–59
    as Creator, 81, 100
    existence of, 83
    faithfulness of, 40
    as field of promise, 84
    and gender, 99–102
    as Monarch, 56, 57, 100
    as personal, 52, 99
    as Spirit, 57
    as Trinity, 59, 102, 152
    See also panentheism; theism

heaven, belief in, viii, ix, 27, 53, 67, 94, 98, 105, 109, 148, 164
hell, belief in, ix, 27, 53, 148, 164
Hillel (rabbi), 66

incarnation, doctrine of, ix, 91–94, 101, 132, 152
independent attestation, criterion of, 112, 114, 116, 117

Jesus, 59, 73, 95, 96, 108, 131, 132, 133–34
    as apocalyptic prophet, 108, 110–12, 115–21, 131, 134
    as the Christ, 91, 92–93
    deity of, ix, 94–95, 133
    ethical teachings of, 118–19, 133–34
    humanity of, 94–95, 96, 98–99
    life of, viii, 83, 112–15, 134, 153
    as Logos, 90
    resurrection of, 122, 132, 152
    as Savior, viii
    Second Coming of, viii, ix, 92, 93, 105–8, 122, 123, 132, 163–65
    as Son of God, 95, 97
    as Son of Man, 95, 97, 117
Joachim of Fiore, 107
John the Baptist, 110, 113, 115, 116, 117, 128
Johnson, Jason, 4
Jones, Jim, 15–17
Jones, Robert, 10
Judas Iscariot, 120
Jung, Carl, viii

kataphatic, 59n18
Kierkegaard, Søren, 23, 78
kingdom of God, ix, 106, 107, 108, 109, 110, 111, 112, 113, 115, 116, 117, 118, 119, 120, 122, 123, 125, 126, 130–33, 149, 150–51, 152, 163, 164, 165
    Jesus' teaching about, 127–30, 131, 151
Knox, John, 98
Kohlberg, Lawrence, 21
Kreeft, Peter, 76–78
Kuhn, Thomas, vii
Küng, Hans, 86

LaHaye, Tim, 166
Lao Tzu, 49
"last-day/end-time" thinking, 14, 105, 126–27, 163–66
Lewis, C. S., 90, 95
Lindsey, Hal, 107, 166
Loftus, John, 18, 131

love, 27, 29, 30, 31, 43, 56, 59, 73, 74, 83, 87, 88, 93, 94, 102
Luther, Martin, 96

Martin, Walter, 14
Matthys, Jan, 165
McLaren, Brian, vii, ix, 22, 23, 43, 45, 85, 132
McLoughlin, William, 137, 138
Merton, Thomas, 102
Michener, James, 49
Mill, John Stuart, 53
millennialism, 123–27, 131, 136, 163–66
　See also amillennialism; dispensationalism; postmillennialism; premillennialism
Miller, William, 107, 136
miracles, belief in, ix, 18
Moltmann, Jürgen, 55
Montanus, 107
Moody, D. L., 166
Mormonism, 14, 18, 19
myth(s), viii, ix, 80, 132

nondualism, vii, viii, 29, 49, 89, 90, 99

Obama, Barak, 1, 9, 10, 12, 138
Origen of Alexandria, 101
orthodoxy
　definition of, 39
Outsider Test for Faith, 18, 20

panentheism, 54–56, 87, 102
paradigm shift, vii, 66, 138
paradoxy, 29
Paul (apostle), 29, 30, 42, 66, 72, 74, 92, 93, 94, 107, 117, 129, 149
Peacocke, Arthur, 55
Pelosi, Nancy, 7
Pence, Michael, 7
Perennial Tradition, 47–49, 50–51
Phillips, J. B., 59
Piaget, Jean, 21
Postcritical Paradigm, 67, 68–69
postmillennialism, 163, 164–65
Powell, Colin, 8

Precritical Paradigm, 67, 68, 95
premillennialism, 105, 163, 165, 166
psychoticism, 6

QAnon, 2

racism, 9, 10, 47, 68, 158
religion, 33–38, 48, 74, 80
　definition of, 33, 36–37, 142–43
　end of, 143–44
　role of, 33, 104
religious, 139–40
Revelation, book of, 104, 123–27, 151, 163, 164
Richardson, Alan, 82
Ricoeur, Paul, 23
Rohr, Richard, 23, 92n2
Russell, Charles Taze, 136

salvation, ix, 105, 106, 125, 126, 138, 145, 149, 152, 159
Satan, satanic, 2, 14, 89, 90, 109, 123, 163, 164, 165
Schweitzer, Albert, 115
Scofield, C. I., 166
Scotus, John Duns, 91
scripture. *See* Bible
Second Coming. *See* Jesus, Second Coming of
sexism, 9, 10, 68, 118, 158
Sheldon, Charles, 133
sin, ix, 57, 85, 105, 109, 151, 159
Smith, Joseph, 18–19
Smith, Wilfred Cantwell, 90, 142
Son of Man (as cosmic figure), 116, 117, 118, 119, 120
Sophia, 101–2
Spaulding, Solomon, 19
spirituality, 21, 30, 72, 80, 93, 139–40, 142, 146
　apophatic, 59n17
　kataphatic, 59n18
Spong, John Shelby, 53, 59, 160n2
Steuco, Agostino, 48

Tao, the, 48, 49, 89, 90
Ten Commandments, 41, 62–63
Tertullian, 107, 165

theism, 52, 54, 55, 94
Tillich, Paul, 58–59
Toynbee, Arnold, 77
True Self, 49, 132
Trump, Donald, 1, 2, 3, 4, 5, 7, 8, 9, 10, 12, 15, 22, 28, 138
trust, 24, 30, 40, 42
truth, 5, 9, 30, 82, 96
    false, 147
    religious, ix, 17–18
    telling, 5

ultimate questions, 40, 48
Universal Christ, the, 92

Weber, Eugen, 106
Whisenant, Edgar, 106
Whitby, Daniel, 165
White, Ellen, 136
Whitehead, Alfred North, 54, 56, 58
Wilber, Ken, 22
wisdom, 76, 101, 147, 148
    See also Sophia

Zakaria, Fareed, 8

www.ingramcontent.com/pod-product-compliance
Lightning Source LLC
Chambersburg PA
CBHW070922180426
43192CB00037B/1676